Contents

Lesson (sight words)

Lesson (sight words)

First Aid for Reading

Sonya Stoneman

Illustrated by Caanan Grall

Pembroke Publishers Limited

Pembroke Publishers
538 Hood Road
Markham, Ontario, Canada L3R 3K9
www.pembrokepublishers.com

Distributed in the U.S. by Stenhouse Publishers
P.O. Box 360
York, Maine 03909
www.stenhouse.com

©1999 Wizard Books Pty Ltd. Originally published in Australia as *First Aid in Reading*

Canadian Cataloguing in Publication Data

Stoneman, Sonya
    First aid for reading: phonics-based activities for struggling readers

Canadian ed.
ISBN 1-55138-113-3

1. Reading (Primary). 2. English language – Phonetics – Problems, exercises,
etc. 3. English language – Phonetics – Study and teaching (Primary).
4. Reading – Remedial teaching. I. Title

LB1525.3.S76 1999   372.46'5   C99-931398-3

Editor for North American edition: Carol-Ann Freeman
Cover Design: John Zehethofer
Cover Photography: Cressaid Media, Ballarat
Original cartoon art: Caanan Grall
Design and typesetting: Leanne Roulston and JayTee Graphics

Printed and bound in Canada
9 8 7 6 5 4 3 2 1

# Introduction

To become independent readers, children need to develop a variety of skills and strategies. One of the most essential is knowledge of the relationship between sounds and letters (phonics). Since 80% of words in the English language follow 'rules' or patterns, children familiar with a wide range of sound-to-letter correspondences have a solid foundation to build on.

First Aid for Reading is a systematic, phonics-based program devised for children who are experiencing reading difficulties. It would also be suitable for those coming to English for the first time, and readers wanting to 'get ahead'. However, it is well suited for use in both primary and secondary schools by teachers involved in remedial programs. Parents and tutors will find *First Aid for Reading* easy to follow, as specific instructions are given in each lesson.

Parents concerned about their child's reading progress could also use this program at home. We suggest that a suitable time be negotiated to suit parent and child. At least two sessions per week are advisable. It is important for parents to be patient and avoid frustrating situations or distractions which could prove negative for the child. Praise should be lavish and frequent.

The Pretest on page 8 has been designed to pinpoint which sounds are causing difficulty. As *First Aid for Reading* is developmental in format, it is recommended that students begin at the page indicated, and then follow the program in sequence. One lesson per session is sufficient. Children overloaded with new material may lose interest and motivation. Progress can be monitored by filling in the Score Card at the back of the book; this will indicate which sounds need revision. When the child has completed the program to a level appropriate for his/her age (as determined by the teacher), repeat the test. We are confident that a real improvement will be evident, providing that the child does not suffer from a severe intellectual or auditory disability.

Although *First Aid for Reading* is phonics-based, students are encouraged to develop other reading strategies such as continuous checking for meaning, re-reading to find context cues, and looking for smaller, known words inside longer ones. It is vital to offer praise when the child realizes an error has been made and self-corrects. It is very important for tutors to talk about letter patterns learned in each lesson and think of similar examples.

Additional exercises, games, and stories have been included to reinforce the sound patterns learned in the lessons. These activities will appeal to children and are easy for a parent to follow. The main focus is on rhyming, which is invaluable in the development of basic literacy skills (reading, writing, and spelling).

Many of the Revision Lessons include the Fish Game. For durability, schools can laminate the cards. Parents may want to photocopy the sheets onto cardboard. Children enjoy playing with these cards, which are valuable as revision and as a reward for good work.

The Story Lessons feature words from the previous set of lessons, but several unfamiliar words may be included to help the child develop a variety of strategies essential for independent reading, such as reading on to find context cues.

To encourage a reluctant child to read a story aloud, read the title and then look at the illustration together. Ask him/her to predict what the story could be about. Have a guess yourself. As the child reads, pause to allow him/her time to problem-solve. Prompt when necessary, for example, "Try to sound out that word.", "Read on to the end of the sentence.", "That word means the same as...", "What word starting with...would make sense?". Praise any self-corrections made and congratulate the child for reading the story all by him/herself.

Included at the end of the book is a full listing of the approximately 2,500 words featured in this program and a Certificate for the student who successfully completes the course.

Good luck and enjoy *First Aid for Reading*!

$\mathscr{P}$retest

For the tutor
1. Sit the student down at a table, away from all noise and distractions.
*2. Ask him/her to read across each line in turn. (You may need to put a bookmark under the line to help him/her focus on the words). Encourage the student to "have a go", but **do not prompt**. Incorrect responses may be tried again.*
3. Circle those words that he/she cannot correctly read.
*4. **When he/she makes three or more errors in a single line, stop the pretest.***

Important Note

Start Here

You have now established (as a rough guide) the level of reading at which the student is experiencing difficulty. The Pretest list is carefully graded, from the simplest reading to the most advanced, and is directly keyed into the program itself.

The number opposite each set of words is the page number for the lesson which deals with that phonic group. The student can begin the program at this point. If other difficulties become apparent, you may need to selectively "visit" other earlier lessons. What each lesson covers is clearly laid out in the Table of Contents.

a e i o u	11
m b n d p	12
fat mug bin fox let van	17
hiss doll puff less fill tell	36
zips eggs pans logs begs cuffs	39
dump junk desk ramp milk lost	44
slap flat club prod brim plum	47
crust stunt slept drank stomp print	50
cash fish shot fresh blush shift	56
thin moth froth throb thrill thump	59
ring hung bring hopping strong skipping	62
rich champ finch punch chest branch	65
after robber sister ladder drummer shelter	70
deck socks smack pluck sticker cricket	73
fall stall malt small taller alter	78
mate rake tame scale crane shakes	82

Lesson 1

For the tutor

*This lesson revises the building blocks of all reading: recognition of the **vowels** (open sounds) and **consonants** (closed sounds).*

Match the following vowel letters to the object which starts with the same sound. (You might need to help him/her with igloo and orange.)

a

e

i

o

u

Now what about the consonant sounds? Match the following letters to words which start with the same sounds.

b

c

d

f

g

h

First Aid for Reading © 1999. Permission for purchaser to copy for non-commercial classroom use. Pembroke Publishers

j

k

l

m

n

p

q

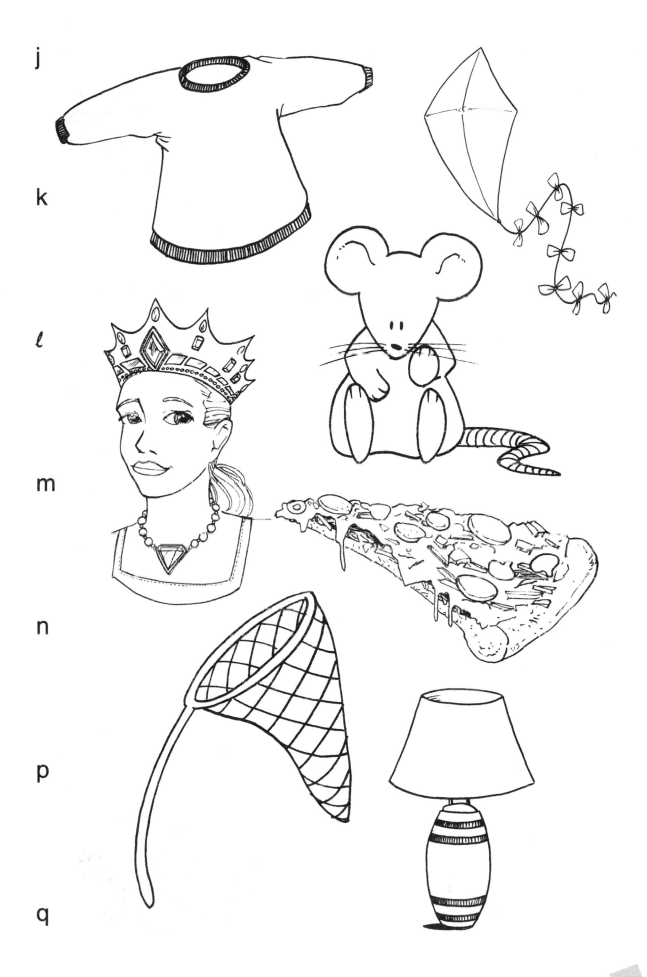

r

s

t

v

w

x

y

z

Excellent. You know the alphabet. All the words in English are made up of these letters. Some of them change their sounds, but don't worry. We will learn how they can be read in different ways later in the program. You know the letters themselves. Let's now start reading them in words.

Fish Game 1

- Photocopy and cut into squares. The aim is to find matching pairs of letters.
- Deal out 6 cards each. Put the remaining cards in a pile between players.
- Have the first go to model the procedure.
- Example: "I have the letter "d", do you have the card that matches?" A correct match earns another turn and returns the matching pair to the pile. An incorrect match loses a turn.
- The player to lose all their cards first, wins.

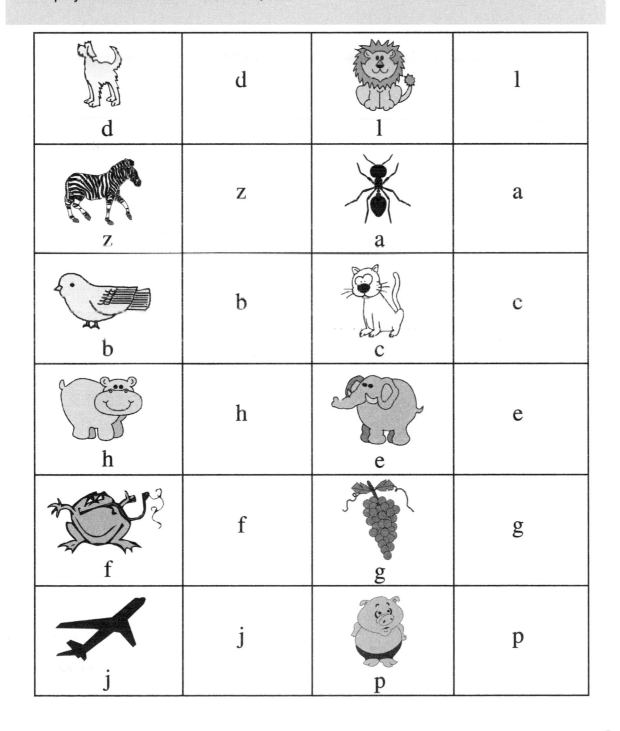

Fish Game 1

k	k	m	m
o	o	r	r
s	s	t	t
n	n	w	w
u	u	v	v
y	y	q	q

Lesson 2

For the tutor

*The goal of this lesson is for your child to master **short vowels** in simple words. What is a short vowel? It is a sound like the "a" in hat, the "e" in bed, the "i" in pig, the "o" in dog, or the "u" in cup. It is very important that he/she pronounces them as short vowels, and **not as long vowels** (like the "a" in hate, the "e" in feet, the "i" in bite, the "o" in snow, or the "u" in cute). This course deliberately starts with the short vowels, and works on them, before complicating things by introducing the long vowels.*

You need to know the sounds made by the short vowels. There are five short vowel sounds. Point to the picture as I say each word.

man

can

pan

bed

net

jet

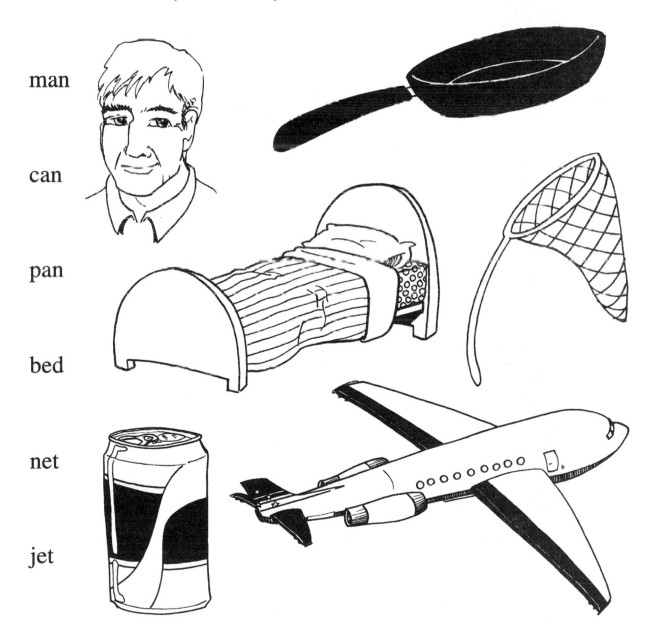

pig

dig

hit

dog

hot

pot

mug

bug

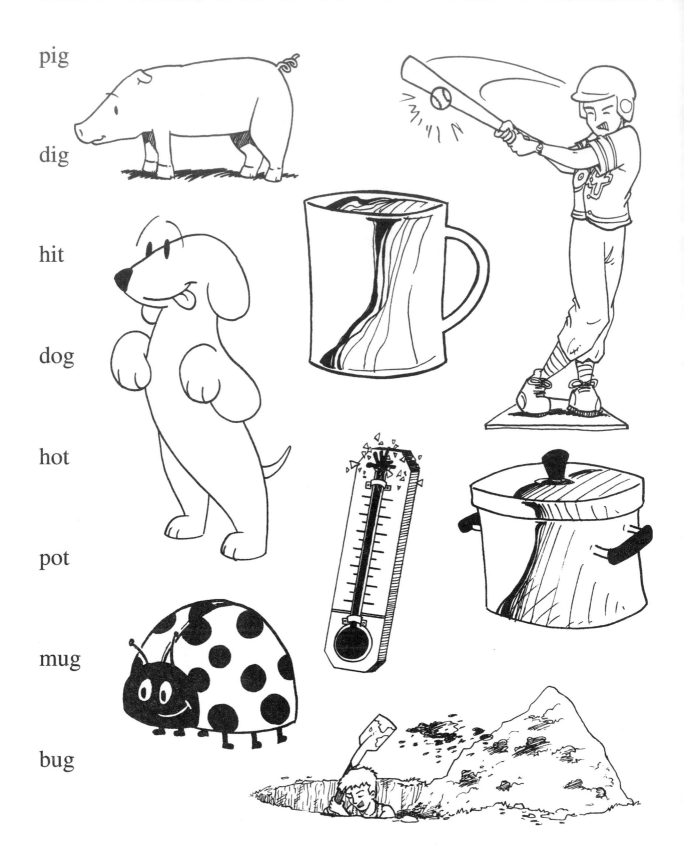

Very good! Now I want *you* to say the word, and point to it, as I point to each picture.
The first letters will help you.

Congratulations!

Now let's try something a little different. Look carefully at the following words (*the first line below, starting with the word dog*). Can you tell me which word has the sound "a", as in "hat"? Take all the time you need. (*Say the words slowly and clearly. Repeat as often as necessary*).

dog fat bin mug

That was excellent! Now see if you can hear the sound "e" (*as in "pet"*).

zip pot peg jam

You did it! What about the sound "i" (*as in "pig"*)?

fun leg fat rod hit

That's right. Now let's try the sound "o" (*as in "hot"*).

tub sip tan get log

Fantastic listening! The last sound is "u" (*as in "nut"*).

pen lid gum hop fat

That was great! Now you can read the five ways the short vowel sounds are normally written.

On a separate piece of paper, draw two of the following words. Label your artwork.

mug pig cap dog pen van box

Lesson 3

For the tutor

The child needs to be able to blend those simple short vowel sounds (as in Lesson 1) and the consonant sounds with which they normally appear. These exercises will help.

Before we start, read the words under the pictures for me.

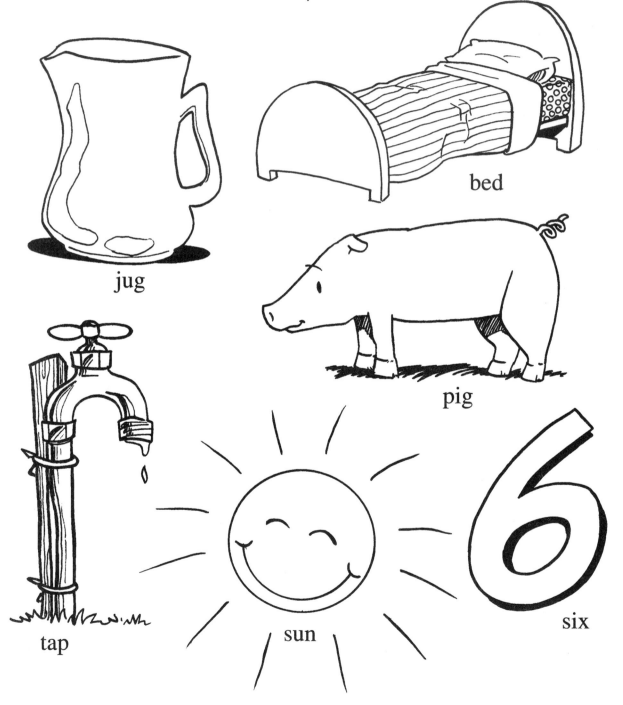

jug

bed

pig

tap

sun

six

That was excellent! Now look at the words in the lists as I read them. (*Say the words very slowly and distinctly.*)

1. Which word has the sound "ap"?

   kid mat map van pop

2. Which word has the sound "et"?

   lip cub hen ban vet

3. Which word has the sound "im"?

   jug get sit bug him

4. Which word has the sound "og"?

   fin gun fog fit nag

5. Which word has the sound "un"?

   jam fan pup bat bun

1. Which word has the sound "ax"?

   fox wax log rip pet

2. Which word has the sound "en"?

   cot fig rub hen lap

3. Which word has the sound "id"?

   rid set ham cop sum

4. Which word has the sound "ob"?

   fat dug rob pin men

5. Which word has the sound "um"?

   cab six got gum nib

My Score ⬚/10

That was amazing!

Lesson 4

For the tutor
This lesson works on the most common three letter words.

Can you read the words under the pictures for me?

fox

pot

cap

rat

pen

bus

Great!

This time I want you to try reading the words in each line yourself. See if you can find and circle the two words that rhyme, like "sit" and "bit", or "mop" and "top". Sound out the letters separately, like this: b - u - n : bun. You will soon be able to join familiar letters to make one sound, like "un", "an", and "in". (*Praise correct attempts.*)

1. bun fat had let tin sun

2. tan box rum nap fox get

3. mat pan sit lap kid fan

4. dog sip lid fed mug fog

5. mix bat log rat bug van

That was really clever! Now I want you to unscramble the letters to make words. The first one is done for you. Make sure you put the vowel in the middle.

1. s n u   sun

2. d d i   _____

3. n a v   _____

4. e g t   _____

5. x o f   _____

Well done!

In the next set, one word in each line is a made-up word. Can you find it and cross it out for me?

1. rat win lot nuz bed

2. jug rob leg man hin

3. pod nag bus lex tip

4. van yod met zip nut

5. mud pet wid fun cop

That was very good reading. In the last set, see if you can add a letter to make a word. There could be more than one answer.

1. __ ug

2. __ et

3. __ ip

4. __ am

5. __ot

My Score /20 Fantastic!

Lesson 5

For the tutor

*The goal of this lesson is for your child to master a number of the most common three letter words based around a short vowel. In addition, we will be revising the basic words **a** and **the**.*

Read the words under the pictures for me again please.

zip

hot

cat

10

ten

hen

bag

Well done! Today we are learning some words that you have to know by sight: "a" and "the" (*point to the words at the top of the page*). Sounding out words like this doesn't help much. We call them "sight" words, because you have to be able to say them on sight. All the other words we will use in the following exercises can be sounded out.

Look at the sentences below. Read each sentence aloud, first with one of the words in brackets, then with the second word in brackets. Which one makes more sense? I'll do the first one for you.

1. The (ten pen) is in the box.

   The ten is in the box. The pen is in the box.

Which makes more sense? It's the pen. Circle "pen" for me. Good! Now you try!

2. A (cat sat) is in the cot.

3. Is a (rat mat) in the jug?

4. The (dig big) man is fat.

5. A (box fox) has the hen.

6. Is the (bed fed) in the van?

7. A (bog dog) is in the bus.

8. Ben had a (lap nap) in the sun.

Excellent reading!

This time I want you to read all the words in the following list and then write down in the space provided the one that fits best in each sentence.

1. The _____ bit Sam on the leg.

2. The pig sat in the _____.

3. The bad _____ is in the bin.

4. Tom has _____ his cap.

5. _____ up the red bag.

6. Did Meg get a _____?

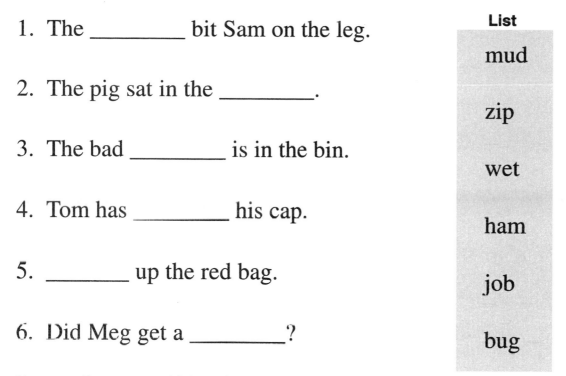

List

mud

zip

wet

ham

job

bug

Now see if you can add the missing letter to make a word that fits the meaning.

1. A f _ x has got the hen.

2. Rod is in the v _ n.

3. A p _ p sat on the log.

4. Jan has fed the c _ t.

5. A lid is on the b _ x.

6. Let Kim get the m _ g.

My Score 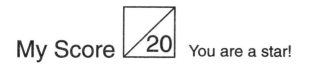 /20 You are a star!

 *Lesson 6*

For the tutor
*This lesson continues work on basic three letter words with a short vowel. In addition, we will be revising the basic words **to**, **do**, **of**, **and**.*

Read the words under the pictures first please.

bin

hat

mug

leg

pen

ram

Good! Today the words to be memorized are "to", "of", "and" and "do" (*point to the words at the top of the page*).

Read the sentences below. Once again, work out which word makes more sense and circle it.

1. The (rap cap) is in the van.

2. Do not pat the (fox box).

3. Is the (kid lid) on the bin?

4. Zip up the old (tag bag).

5. Do not sit in the hot (bun sun).

6. Get us a pot of (dam jam).

7. Let the vet do his (job gob).

8. Liz has a bad cut on the (lip sip).

Wonderful!

Read the words and write in the one that fits best.

List

1. Mum has a red _____.

    ran

2. The _____ is big and fat.

    bit

3. Six men _____ to get the bus.

    fix

4. Do not let the _____ get hot.

    ram

5. The dog _____ the big rat.

    hat

6. Sam has to _____ the zip.

    wax

Good!

Now add the missing letters.

1. Ken has cut his l _ g.

2. Do not let the pig get f _ t.

3. Put the old pen in the b _ n.

4. The c _ p has a rip in it.

5. Get a pin to f _ x the hem.

6. Bob sat in the s _ n and got hot.

My Score ⟋ 20

SHORT "a"

- Say the words. Cross out the ones that do not belong.
- Join the words that rhyme with a line. The first one is done for you.

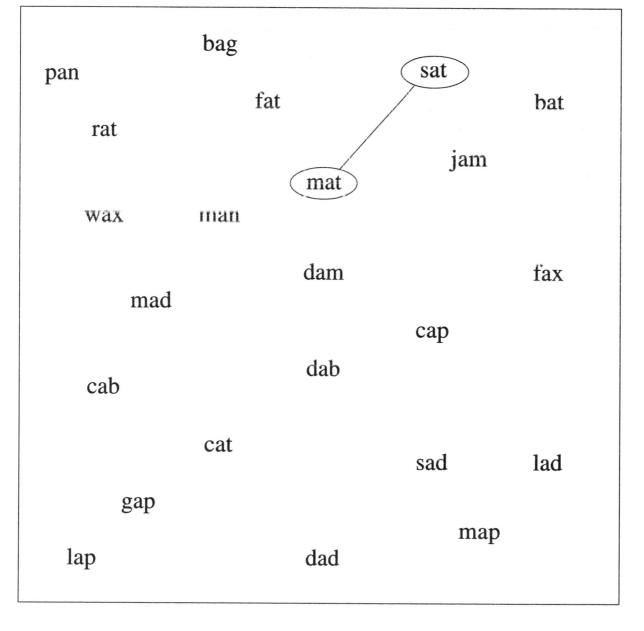

bag

pan

fat   (sat)   bat

rat

jam

(mat)

wax   man

dam   fax

mad

cap

dab

cab

cat

sad   lad

gap

map

lap   dad

Revision Lessons 2-6

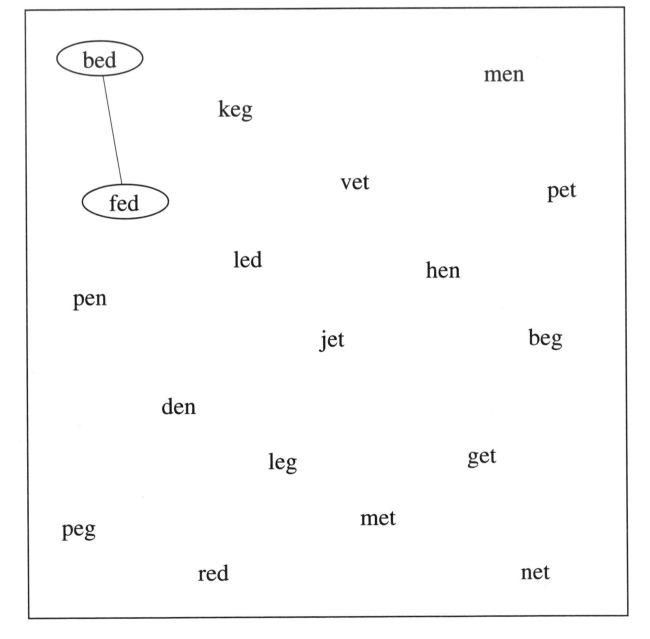

bed

men

keg

vet

pet

fed

led

hen

pen

jet

beg

den

leg

get

peg

met

red

net

SHORT "i"

- Say the words. Cross out the ones that do not belong.
- Join the words that rhyme with a line. The first one is done for you.

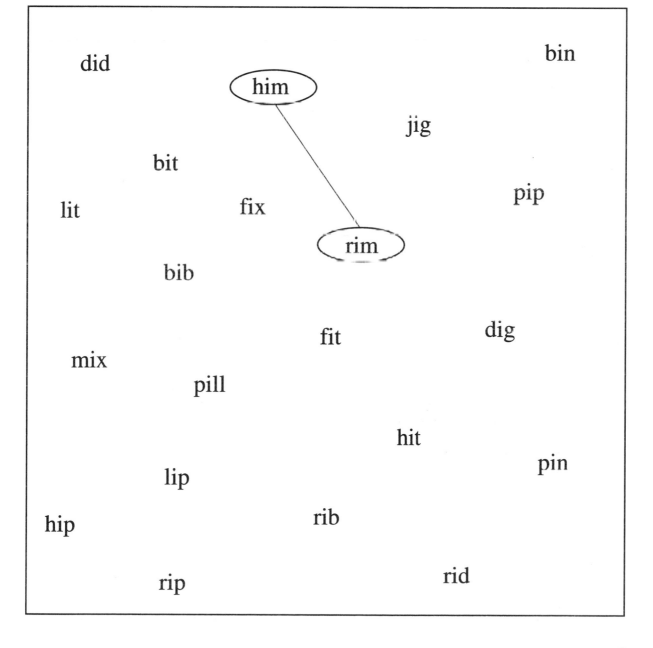

did

bin

him

jig

bit

pip

lit   fix

rim

bib

fit   dig

mix

pill

hit

pin

lip

hip   rib

rip   rid

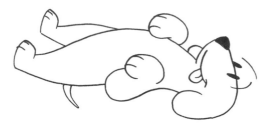

SHORT "o"

• Say the words. Cross out the ones that do not belong.
• Join the words that rhyme with a line. The first one is done for you.

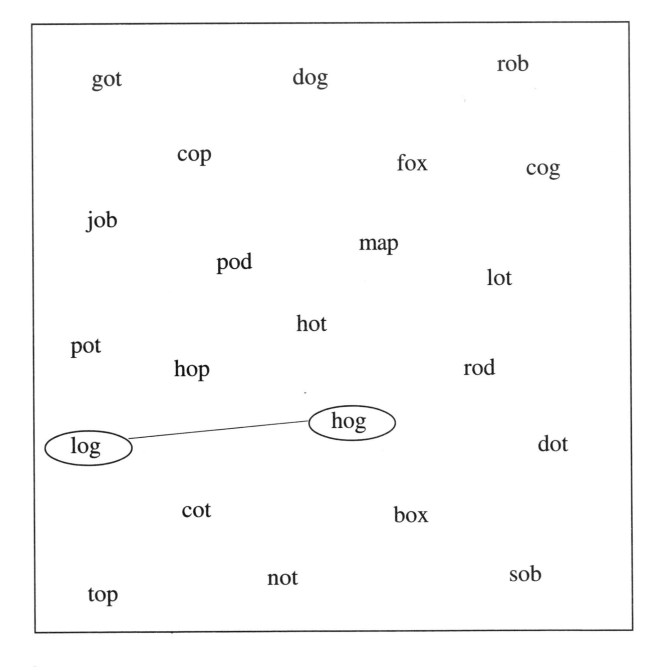

got   dog   rob

cop   fox   cog

job   map

pod   lot

hot

pot   rod

hop

(log)——(hog)   dot

cot   box

not   sob

top

SHORT "u"

• Say the words. Cross out the ones that do not belong.
• Join the words that rhyme with a line. The first one is done for you.

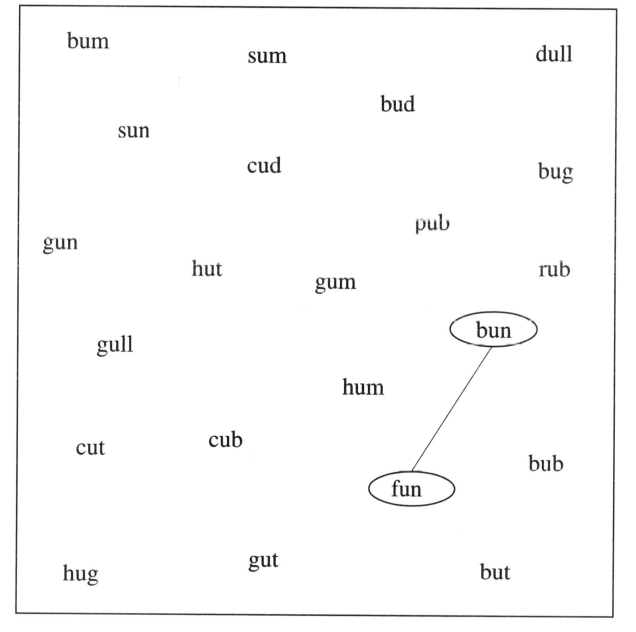

bum

sum   dull

bud

sun

cud   bug

pub

gun

hut   rub

gum

bun

gull

hum

cut   cub

bub

fun

hug   gut   but

Double consonants

This lesson teaches you the double consonant sounds, like those under the pictures (*point*). Double consonants sound exactly the same as single consonants. Read them to me please.

mess

putt

hiss

kiss

mutt

Terrific!

Now read the words in each line. Can you find the rhyming pairs and circle them?
(*Praise correct attempts. If necessary, model how to sound out the words: f-e-l-l, f-ell, and explain what "rhyme" means.*)

1. fell cuff fizz sell biff

2. boss doll fill mess will

3. miss puff bell kill kiss

4. mutt cuff miss well duff

5. tell buzz toss moss less

Good work!

Now I want you to unscramble the letters to make real words. The double consonant goes at the end.

Read the words.

1. f f i b _____

2. o l d l _____

3. m s e s _____

4. e b l l _____

5. l s s a _____

Fantastic!

There is a made-up word in each line below. Cross it out.

1. miss buzz cuff lass bixx

2. fizz puff rebb less putt

3. mutt mass hill kohh toss

4. vidd less bill roll biff

5. jumm fell moss kill mess

Well done!

See if you can add a letter in the space to make a word.

1. ___ oss

2. __izz

3. __uff

4. __ess

5. __ill

My Score /20 You did it!

Lesson 8

Using the letter "s"
sight words:
are you I be me we he

For the tutor

*The letter "s" can be used at the end of a verb, or "doing word". It is also used to make a plural, that is, **more than one** of something. Read the picture words to see what I mean.*

runs

dogs

eggs

hens

hats

mops

That was easy, wasn't it? Look at the sight words above. You need to be able to read them without thinking.

Now try these sentences for me.

1. (Ten Hen) pins are in the red box.

2. Bill and Max are at the (mill dill).

3. Toss six (legs eggs) into the pan.

4. Tell Ross to cut up the (dogs logs).

5. Are the (pigs figs) in the pen yet?

Good work! Read the list of words and write in the one that makes sense.

List

1. Mum _____ up the mess.

he

2. I yell and the cat _____ to me.

nips

3. Jill has _____ old dolls.

runs

4. Will _____ be on the bus?

mops

5. The bad pup _____ at the hens.

some

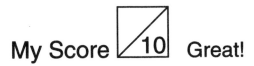

My Score ___/10 Great!

Now choose the word in brackets that fits best.

1. Did you hear the (loss bell) ring?

2. The fat (figs pigs) sat in the mud.

3. The boss cut his (legs begs) at the mill.

4. You can not kiss me on the (zips lips).

5. The red (pens hens) are in the bin.

Way to go! Now see if you can add the missing letters. (Clue: All the words have double consonants.)

1. Do we get hot r   lls at ten?

2. Jess will get wet cu _ fs.

3. The man s _ lls cans of wax.

4. Did a fox get the eg _ s?

5. Did you m _ ss the bus?

Super reading!

My Score   /10

Max

Max is my pet. He is a <u>black</u> and tan pup. Dad got him for me at the pub.

Max can be a mutt. He rolls in the mud with the pigs and nips at the hens. He rips the mats into bits. He wets on Mum's legs.

Mum gets <u>cross</u> and tells Max he is a bad pup, but he is my pal. He sits on my bed and <u>licks</u> me till I get up. We go off and <u>play</u> in the sun. Max is a lot of fun!

The words underlined are new. If your child has difficulty with them, the prompts below should help (or use your own).

<u>black</u>: Read to the end of the sentence...This word describes the pup; it is a color starting with the letter "b".

<u>cross</u>: Read the second paragraph again...How would Mum feel when Max does these naughty things? Would she be pleased?

<u>licks</u>: Read on. What might a puppy do to get you out of bed?...He does it with his tongue.

<u>play</u>: Read on to the end of the story... What word starting with "p" would make sense?

Join up the words that rhyme.

kiss	bell
loss	rugs
bin	pans
sell	hiss
fox	din
mugs	get
cap	fix
vans	boss
let	box
mix	map

Read the sentences below. Put a tick next to the sentences which *could* be true, and a cross next to the sentences which *could not* be true.

1. A fox can kill a rat.

2. I will kiss the fat hog.

3. The mess is in the garbage.

4. A pup fell in the well.

5. A cat can fix the bell.

6. Nan puffs up the hill.

That was excellent reading! Now draw a picture in the box above to illustrate one of the sentences.

 *Lesson 9*

For the tutor

This lesson is about words ending with a blend of consonants, that is, two or more consonants next to each other. You need to practise joining the sounds of the letters together like this: m-i-l-k, m-il-k.

Try the picture words first.

milk

jump

cold

drum

tent

hand

lift

Well done! Today's sight words are "have", "they", "was", and "give".

Can you circle the correct word in brackets?

1. Kim was (lost cost) in the fog.

2. Jeff and Sam (bent went) on a run.

3. The pins (must bust) not get wet.

4. A bug was on the (junk bunk) bed.

5. Will I be (fold cold) at the camp?

Great! Now read the list of words. See if you can work out which word makes sense and write it in the space for me.

List

1. Is the tire _____ in the car?

limp

2. The _____ bit me on the hand.

milk

3. Can Dad mend the old _____ ?

tent

4. They left a bit of _____ in the jug.

pest

5. The old man has a bad _____ .

pump

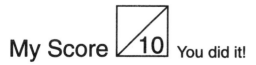

My Score /10 You did it!

Here are more words using a blend of consonants. Choose the correct word in brackets. Make sure the sentence makes sense.

1. (Jump Dump) the mess at the curb.

2. Ross has to (end mend) the desk.

3. The pots and pans are in the (sink pink).

4. We have to (yelp help) at the mill.

5. An old man puffs up the (ramp lamp).

Terrific! Can you add the missing letters? It is a good idea to read the whole sentence first to find meaning clues.

1. Nan had a r _ st on the bed.

2. You m _ st not bend the disk.

3. Can you give me a l _ ft in the van?

4. Mum s _ nt me to get the milk.

5. Don lets me h _ ld his pet rats.

My Score ⟋10 Great work!

 First Aid for Reading © 1999. Permission for purchaser to copy for non-commercial classroom use. Pembroke Publishers

Lesson 10

For the tutor

The lesson today is about words starting with a blend of consonants. You need to practise joining the sounds of the letters together like this: c-r-a-b, cr-ab. Read the picture words and you will see what I mean.

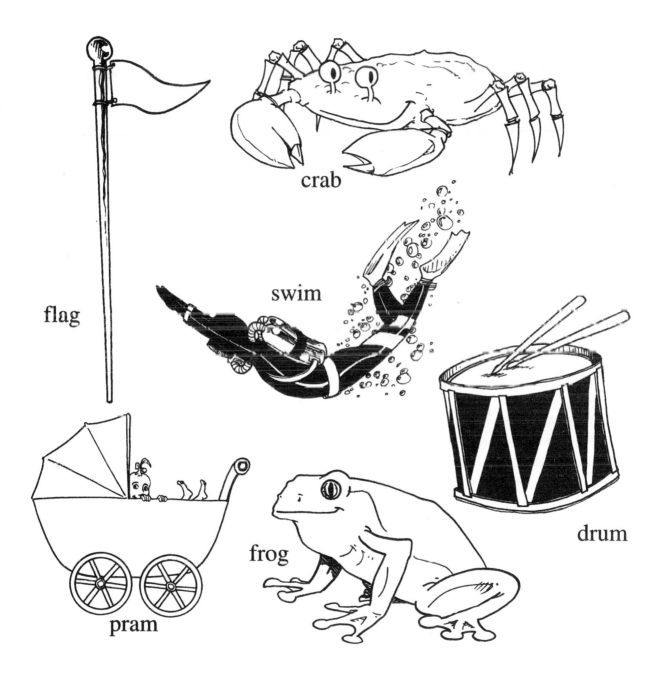

flag

crab

swim

drum

pram

frog

Today's sight words are "by", "my", "go", "no", and "so".

Now choose the correct word in brackets.

1. (Drag Brag) the bad dog up the hill.

2. Give me the best (plum slum) jam.

3. We went on a (grip trip) to the store.

4. Did the bus (stop clop) at the club?

5. Rob left my drum on the (tram cram).

Very good! Now you can complete the sentences, using the words in the list below.

1. We can have no pets at the _____ .

2. Fill the mugs up to the _____ .

3. Can the pup _____ in the pond?

4. A _____ will jump if you prod it.

5. Dad must mend the rips in the _____.

List

swim

flat

brim

flag

frog

 My Score ⊠/10 Great!

Here are more examples of words starting with a blend of consonants. Complete the sentences for me please.

1. Toss my rag dolls in the (tram pram).

2. Mum has a (flan plan) to get slim.

3. Let the (crab grab) go in the pond.

4. We can get off at the next (slop stop).

5. Jeff has a wet (spot slot) on his cuff.

You are doing really well! See if you can add the missing letters. You may need to read the whole sentence to find meaning clues.

1. Dr _ p the rag in the garbage as you go by.

2. Can you get the red top to sp _ n?

3. Give the brat a sl _ p on his leg.

4. The pod will sn _ p if you bend it.

5. I was so gl _ d I had the top bunk at camp.

My Score ⬜/10 Very good reading!

Lesson 11

Initial *and* final blends
sight words:
any many some come

For the tutor

This time you will be reading words with a blend of consonants at the beginning and end. Read the picture words first for some examples.

stamp

plant

drunk

slept

print

drank

Great! The sight words are "any" and "many". It is important to be able to recognize both words.

Now choose the word in brackets that makes sense. Try to join the letters to make sounds, for example, s-t-a-m-p, then st-am-p.

1. Get a (stamp scamp) from the desk.

2. You can (crust trust) me to do any job.

3. A cat (swept crept) up to the nest.

4. Do not (stand brand) on the damp rug.

5. Fred (frank drank) some milk from the jug.

Very good. Now complete the sentences below, using the words in the list.

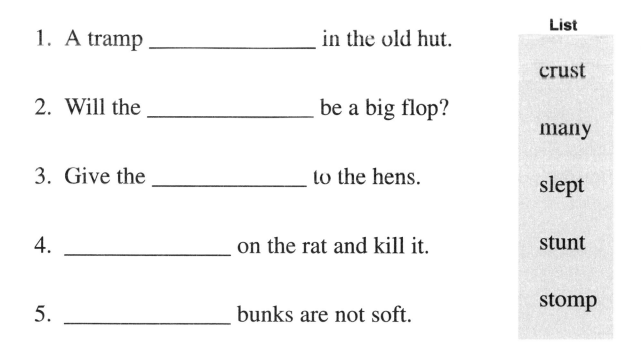

List

1. A tramp _____ in the old hut.

crust

2. Will the _____ be a big flop?

many

3. Give the _____ to the hens.

slept

4. _____ on the rat and kill it.

stunt

5. _____ bunks are not soft.

stomp

My Score  /10

You are doing really well with these longer words. Here are some more examples. See if you can work out which word in brackets makes sense.

1. A man will come to (grand brand) the pigs.

2. I will give Mum a pot (plant slant).

3. Can he (crank prank) up the pump?

4. Ann (swept slept) dust from the tent.

5. Sit on the (clank plank) next to him.

Well done! Now try to fill in the missing letters below. You may need to read to the end of the sentence to find meaning clues.

1. Do not sta _ d on the desk.

2. My pup is a bit of a sc _ mp.

3. Will the hens have m _ ny eggs?

4. Do you have a st _ mp?

5. We can pr _ nt from the disk.

My Score ☐/10 Excellent work!

Revision Lessons 9-11

Unscramble the letters to make words.

upb	p__b	dmu	m__d
dba	ba__	its	__it
etw	w__t	cta	__ __t
pot	t__p	dki	k__ __
smat	m__ts	csot	co__s
psin	pi__s	bsit	b__ts
msus	s__ms	wset	wet__

Unscramble the words to make sentences.

1. in bed is Jeff. _____

2. doll Pam a has. _____

3. in fell I the mud. _____

4. will the Dad rats kill. _____

5. of full eggs is bag The. _____

Write captions under the pictures.

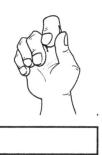

Grant and the Fox

Grant met a red fox on top of a hill.

"Do you have any cubs?" he said.

"Yes, I have six," said the fox. She ran into her den.

Grant told his Dad. Dad went to grab his gun.

"I must kill the fox," he said.

"But the fox has six cubs," Grant wept.

"You are too soft," said his Dad. "The fox will get my hens. We will have no eggs."

Grant ran up to the den.

"You must go. My Dad will come with his gun," he told the fox.

The fox and her cubs ran into the hills. Grant was so glad!

Fish Game 2

- Photocopy and cut into squares. The aim is to find rhyming pairs.
- Deal out six cards each. Put remaining cards in a pile between players.
- Have the first go to model procedure.
- Example: "I have mice, do you have the word that rhymes?" A correct match earns another turn and returns the matching pair to the pile. An incorrect match loses a turn.
- The player to lose all their cards first, wins.

sink	wink	jump	bump
lost	cost	fist	list
clap	slap	clop	slop
flag	clag	plum	slum
crept	swept	stamp	clamp
skunk	spunk	drink	stink

For the tutor

In this lesson, you will learn how to read words with the sound "sh". Read the picture words for some examples.

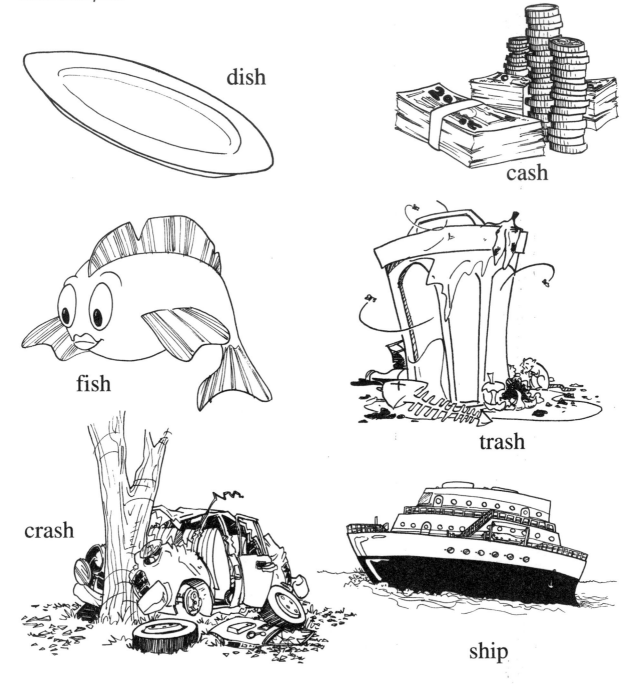

dish

cash

fish

trash

crash

ship

Right. The sight words today are "here", "there", and "put". You need to be able to recognize them.

Now, try the sentences below. Make sure they make sense. (*If necessary, model how to sound out the words, for example, c-a-s-h, c-ash*).

1. Ross spent his (cash lash) on pens.

2. Get some (fish dish) at the shop.

3. Dad (shot shut) the fox in its den.

4. Is (here there) any milk lcft in the jug?

5. We went on a trip in a (shop ship).

Way to go! Now add the missing words.

1. I must _____ to the bank.

2. _____ the plants in the shed.

3. The shop will _____ at six.

4. Put the crusts on a flat _____ .

5. It is _____ to jump off a cliff.

List

put

shut

rush

rash

dish

My Score ◻/10 Great reading!

These words are a bit more difficult because they have a blend of consonants or double consonants.

Words ending with "sh" and "ss" can be made plural by adding "es", for example, **brushes** and **kisses**.

1. Toss the junk into the (trash slash) can.

2. Josh will (plush blush) if you kiss him.

3. Did the bus (crash clash) in the mist?

4. Some (flesh fresh) eggs are in the dish.

5. Put the (crushes brushes) on the sink.

Terrific! Lastly, add the missing letters. You may need to read to the end of the sentence to find meaning clues.

1. Help me sh _ ft the sand into the shed.

2. The pigs sit in the mud and sl _ sh.

3. Brad swept the egg s _ ells into the bin.

4. Are there any pegs on the top sh _ lf?

5. The big frogs spl _ sh into the pond.

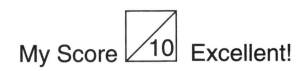

My Score /10 Excellent!

 First Aid for Reading © 1999. Permission for purchaser to copy for non-commercial classroom use. Pembroke Publishers

Lesson 13

For the tutor
This lesson is about words using the sound "th".

Read the picture words for me.

moth

thug

think

thin

thank

broth

Correct! Today's sight words are "our", "your", and "wash" (point).

Underline the word in brackets that makes sense. (If necessary, model how to sound out words: th-e-n, th-en, then).

1. Give the (then thin) dog some scraps.

2. Did (that than) shop sell fresh fish?

3. Wash the dish (pith with) a damp rag.

4. There is a (moth mutt) on your brush.

5. Do not let the (drug thug) get our cash.

Very good! Now write the correct word in the space provided.

1. A box fell off the shelf with a _____ .

List

2. _____ the slush off the van.

Cath

thud

3. Did _____ shell many nuts?

that

4. Get some milk, _____ fill the jugs.

wash

5. Put your trash in _____ red bin.

then

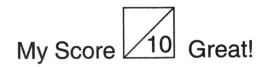

My Score ◻/10 Great!

Here are some more examples of words using "th". They are a little more difficult because they have a blend of consonants or double consonants. Choose the correct word from those in brackets to complete the sentence. (*You may need to explain that thrush is a kind of bird.*)

1. The (thump thrush) has eggs in its nest.

2. Our legs (throb thrill) if we crush them.

3. Is there any (brush broth) left in the pot?

4. Wash the dish with this soft (cliff cloth).

5. I (think thank) I have lost the best disks.

Way to go! Now try to add the missing letters. You may need to read to the end of the sentence to find meaning clues.

1. There was a th _ ft at the bank.

2. A trip on a big ship is a thr _ ll.

3. Seth has lots of fr _ th in his mug.

4. Th _ mp your tin drum in the shed.

5. A bad man will thr _ sh his dogs.

My Score ⬜/10 Very good reading!

First Aid for Reading © 1999. Permission for purchaser to copy for non-commercial classroom use. Pembroke Publishers

For the tutor

This lesson will help you read words using the letter combinations "ang", "ing", "ong", and "ung".
Read the picture words first to see some examples.

fangs

sting

strong

fishing

Good! The sight words are "she", "they", and "want". You need to be able to recognize them.

Now underline the word in brackets that makes sense. (*If necessary, model how to sound out words: s-ing: sing; s-e-v-e-n, s-ev-en*).

1. Did the men (sing ring) in the bus?

2. Max (fang rang) the bell as a prank.

3. Have they (hung rung) up the wet pants yet?

4. They want to go on a (long song) trip.

5. The (ding king) has a dish of broth.

That wasn't hard, was it? Now choose the correct word from the list and write it in. Remember, it must make sense.

1. That old rat has big _____ .

2. Do not _____ on your drum!

3. Will the _____ ring at seven?

4. I wish I had _____ !

5. Did the bee _____ Robbie?

List

sting

bang

fangs

gong

wings

My Score ☐/10 Keep it up!

If you add "ing" to a verb, or doing word, it shows that something is happening right now. The letter combination "ng" can also be used with consonant blends to make interesting words. Look back at the pictures on page 62 to see what I mean.

Can you underline the word in brackets that makes sense?

1. (Bring Fling) me a cup of cold milk.

2. I want a go on the (sting swing).

3. Brett is (slipping skipping) in the slush.

4. Can I come (hopping shopping) with you?

5. Let us go (fishing wishing) in the pond.

Excellent! Now add the missing letters. You may need to read to the end of the sentence to find meaning clues.

1. This spri _ g will rust if it gets wet.

2. Mum cannot h _ ng up the washing.

3. A str _ ng man is lifting up the big ram.

4. Fix up the planks with this stri _ g.

5. Frogs are spl _ shing in the pond.

Count up the number of letters in the last word you completed.

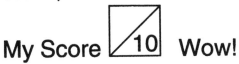

My Score ☐/10 Wow!

Lesson 15

For the tutor

In this lesson, we will be learning the sound "ch". Look at the picture words to see some examples.

chips

chat

lunch

chimp

chest

The sight words today are "one", "two", and "ask". First, underline the word in brackets that makes sense. *(If necessary, model how to sound out words, for example, r-i-c-h, r-ich).*

1. The (rich such) man wants to be king.

2. Glenn had a long (chap chat) with us.

3. I want two big bags of (ships chips).

4. Ask if we can (chop shop) up the plank.

5. Our (chin chess) set is kept in a box.

Good reading! Now choose the correct word from the list and write it in. Remember, it must make sense.

<table>
<tr><td>1. Dad is a _____ at tennis and golf.</td><td rowspan="6">List

chin

champ

lunch

ranch

much</td></tr>
<tr><td>2. Bring me as _____ cash as you can.</td></tr>
<tr><td>3. Are there any pets at the _____ ?</td></tr>
<tr><td>4. Have they rung the _____ bell yet?</td></tr>
<tr><td>5. Grant has a red spot on his _____ .</td></tr>
</table>

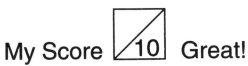

My Score ⬜/10 Great!

Words ending with the sound "ch" can be made plural by adding "es", for example, one **finch**, two **finches**.

1. The thug wants to (finch pinch) our cash.

2. That (bunch stench) comes from the dump.

3. A dog bit a (chink chunk) from my leg.

4. Can I have two drinks of (lunch punch)?

5. We had to dig (trenches drenches) at camp.

Very good! Now write in the missing letters. You may need to read the whole sentence to find meaning clues. (*Explain that the letter "a" at the start or end of a word can have a short "u" sound as in "along".*)

1. They are m _ nching some hot chips.

2. Put your cash in a strong ch _ st.

3. Our old van is c _ ugging up the hill.

4. The c _ apel bells will ring at two.

5. Ch _ mps are swinging from the branches.

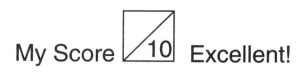

My Score ⟋10 Excellent!

Fish and Chips

"Can we have fish and chips for lunch?" said Cath.

"Yes," said Mum. "Go to the shop with this cash."

It was wet, so Cath ran to the shop.

"I want a big bag of chips, six bits of fish and a drink," Cath told the man in the shop. "Is the fish fresh?"

"This fish is just off the ship," said the man.

Cath put the things in the shopping bag and went home.

"Is the fish fresh?" Mum said with a sniff. "What is that smell?"

She put the fish in the trash bin.

"We will have chips for lunch," she said.

Using "sh"

Draw a line to join the word with the picture, then write the word underneath. Say all the words.

ship

cash

shop

shell

fish

"th"

Circle the words that start or end with "th". Say all the words.

that
tank
plop
with
ship
thin
risk
shot
thump
throb

Draw a thin man

"ch"

Circle the words that start or end with "ch". Say the words.

ships
rich
chop
much
bless
finch
punch
slam
chimp
bunch

Draw a chimp

Lesson 16

For the tutor
Today we will be learning the sound "er". Read the picture words.

bath

ladder

clippers

hammer

thunder

summer

jumper

Good. The sight words today are "bath", "path", and "after" (point). They have a different vowel sound. You need to be able to recognize these words.

Now read the sentences and underline the words in brackets that make sense. (*If necessary, model how to sound out words, for example, r-o-bb-er-s, r-obb-er-s*).

1. Can we go shopping (after rafter) lunch?

2. Frogs are swimming in that (liver river).

3. A finch is hopping on the (path bath).

4. Two (dobbers robbers) hid under the bed.

5. Frank sent them a long (letter better).

That wasn't hard, was it? Now write in the word that matches the meaning of the sentence.

List

1. _____ was chatting to us.

sister

2. I hit my finger with the _____ .

jumper

3. Do you think the punch is _____ ?

bitter

4. Mum put the _____ in the wash.

hammer

5. Tom is stronger than his _____ .

Chester

My Score ⬜/10 Excellent reading!

Once again, read the sentences and underline the words in brackets that make sense.

1. Is the step (ladder madder) under the shelf?

2. Put the old (gunners runners) into the trash.

3. Chop the branch with the (clippers hammers).

4. This band has two (drummers summers).

5. Casper has lost his red (slippers flippers).

Good reading. Now add the missing letters. You may need to read the whole sentence to find meaning clues.

1. Mix some milk and eggs in the bl _ nder.

2. Can Bert and Tom have s _ pper with us?

3. Lester has a big blist _ r on his finger.

4. The sli _ pers are kept in the closet beside the shoes.

5. You must shelter if there is thund _ r.

My Score ⧄ /10 You are a star!

Lesson 17

For the tutor

A blend of the letters "c" and "k" always makes the sound "k". Read the picture words first to see what I mean.

clock

kick

cricket

lock

duck

Well done. The sight words are "boy", "girl", and "were" (point). They are important words for you to remember.

Please read the sentences and underline the words in brackets that make sense. (*If necessary, model how to sound out words, for example, s-t-u-ck, st-uck*).

1. Put the dishes onto a (rack jack).

2. Rex was (sick kick), but his sister was sicker.

3. One (tuck duck) is swimming in the river.

4. Wash your (socks locks) in the sink.

5. A boy ran along the (neck deck) of the ship.

Very good. Now choose the word that fits in the space. Remember, it must make sense.

List

1. A _____ is slipping in the mud.

2. Some girls were _____ on the cliff.

3. Your _____ jumper is in the wash.

4. Our _____ fell off the bench.

5. _____ the nuts with this hammer.

stuck

black

clock

crack

truck

My Score ◢/10 Excellent reading!

There are lots of interesting words using the sound "ck". Complete the sentences in the usual way.

1. The boys have (slack black) runners.

2. (Smack Stick) two stamps on this letter.

3. (Stack Stuck) the clippers in the chest.

4. That was such a clever (brick trick)!

5. Hens were (clucking plucking) in the pen.

Terrific work! Now add the missing letters. You may need to read the whole sentence to find meaning clues.

1. A cl _ ck is ticking at the back of the shop.

2. Six crack _ rs are on the top shelf.

3. Do the girls want some frog stic _ ers?

4. Beth and Jack are at the cri _ ket game with Dad.

5. Can I get two p _ ckets of chips for lunch?

My Score ◻/10 You are making excellent progress!

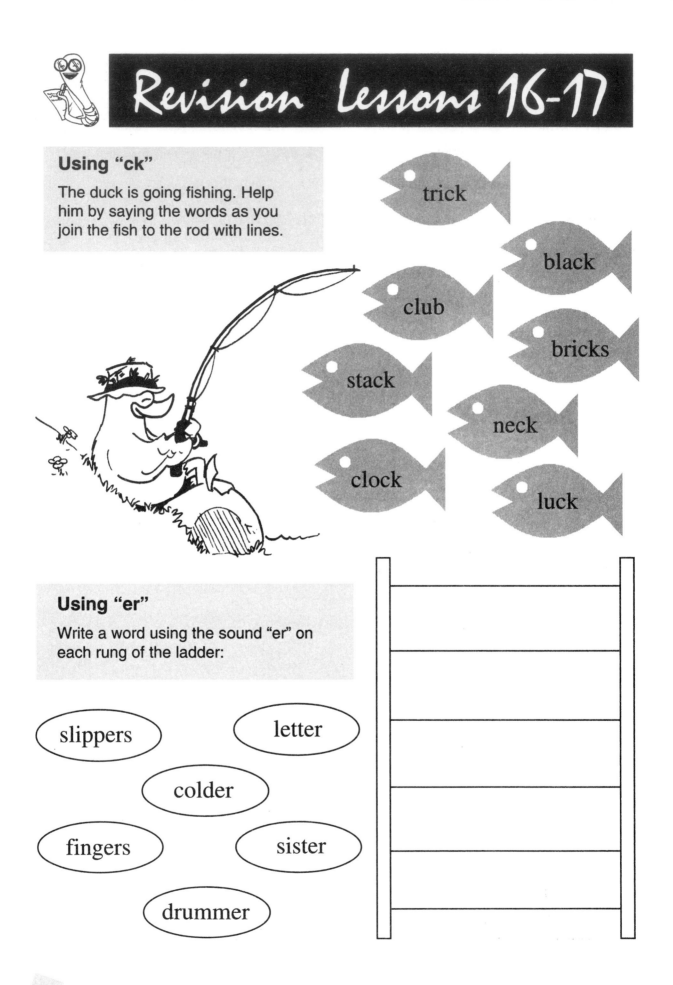

Revision Lessons 16-17

Using "ck"

The duck is going fishing. Help him by saying the words as you join the fish to the rod with lines.

trick

black

club

bricks

stack

neck

clock

luck

Using "er"

Write a word using the sound "er" on each rung of the ladder:

slippers

letter

colder

fingers

sister

drummer

Fish Game 3

- Photocopy and cut into squares. The aim is to find rhyming pairs.
- Deal out 6 cards each. Put the remaining cards in a pile between players.
- Have the first go to model the procedure.
- Example: "I have mice, do you have the word that rhymes?" A correct match earns another turn and returns the matching pair to the pile. An incorrect match loses a turn.
- The player to lose all their cards first, wins.

ball	fall	tall	small
cracker	tracker	clock	block
camp	champ	hopping	chopping
froth	broth	brush	crush
chips	lips	chest	rest
fishing	wishing	ship	lip

Lesson 18

Using "all" and "al"
sight words:
other mother brother another

For the tutor

Today's lesson is about the letter combinations "all" and "al". "al" is usually pronounced "ol", as in "salt". The sight words are "other", "mother", "brother", and "another" (point). They are all important words to learn.

Read the picture words first.

tall

wall

salt

small

calling

Try to work out which words in brackets fit best. (*If necessary, model how to sound out words, for example, c-r-i-ck-e-t, cr-ick-et*).

1. (All Call) my sisters are tennis champs.

2. Mack has a cricket (tall ball) in his hand.

3. Were the (mother other) girls swimming?

4. Do not (fall hall) off that stepladder!

5. We went shopping in the (mall wall).

That was great! Now choose the words that make sense and write them in the spaces.

1. Jock is ____________ than his father.

2. Will the truck ____________ on the hill?

3. A ____________ black duck is in the pond.

4. Is that your ____________ calling you?

5. Get me the ____________ soccer ball.

List

small

taller

other

stall

brother

My Score /10 Well done!

Here are some more words to try.

1. Can I have a (stall small) drink of milk?

2. Josh put (malt salt) and pepper on his chips.

3. Our (other mother) was struck on the leg.

4. I hit the cricket (balls falls) into the net.

5. Put (another brother) plank on the stack.

Good work! Finally, add the missing letters. You may need to read the whole sentence to find meaning clues.

1. Have they come to inst _ ll the pump?

2. Your brother is much small _ r than you.

3. A number of mugs have fal _ en off the bench.

4. Can I have an _ ther jumper?

5. Ask the man in the shop to alt _ r your ring.

My Score ☐/10 That was wonderful!

Chester the Chimp

Chester is a chimp. He lives in the forest with his mother and two brothers, Rick and Josh. Their father was shot by a hunter when they were small.

Chester and his brothers have fun all day long. They swing from the branches and run along the path, hunting for interesting things to play with. Then they collect nuts for supper. As the shells are too hard to crack by hand, they smash them with a rock.

After supper, the chimps go to sleep in a nest of twigs and branches where the hunters cannot see them.

Lesson 19

For the tutor

At the very beginning of this program, we learned to read simple three letter words – consonant plus vowel plus consonant. The vowels in these words were short (e.g. mat, cat, hat). However, when a final e is added, look what happens. Before starting these exercises, play Fish Game 4 on page 94 to demonstrate how the long vowel pattern works.

mat   add an "e"   **mate**

man   add an "e"   **mane**

A final e is almost always silent – *but* it changes the preceding vowel to a long vowel, that is, the name of the letter. See if you can choose the correct word:

1. Mum (mad made) us hot dogs for lunch.

2. Is that a (rat rate) on the bench?

3. Jack met his best (mat mate) at the hockey game.

4. The jumper will (fad fade) in the hot sun.

5. (Sam Same) put salt on his fish and chips.

Fill in the gaps using the words in the list.

List

late

lake

tame

rake

take

1. I must not _____ the dog to the shops.

2. Mother let me swim in the _____.

3. Justin has a _____ rabbit for a pet.

4. Put the _____ back in the shed.

5. My brother was _____ for the bus.

My Score ☐/10

Read the words under the pictures below. They all have the long "a" sound.

plane

plate

snake

skate

Now see if you can choose the correct words.

1. Put all the cakes on this (plate slate).

2. Do not stand on the black (stake snake)!

3. Toss the (stale scale) buns in the garbage can.

4. Robert went on a long (plane plate) trip.

5. Can I have a go on your (scales skates)?

That was super! Now try to write in the missing letters. You may need to read the whole sentence to find meaning clues.

16. Brett wants a pl _ te of pasta for dinner.

17. My pl _ ne ticket is still in my pocket.

18. Dad sh _ kes salt and pepper on his chops.

19. St _ ke the plant with this long stick.

20. Can the cran _ pick up the big crates?

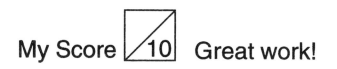

My Score ⬚/10 Great work!

Lesson 20

For the tutor
Read the words under the pictures below. They all have the long "i" sound.

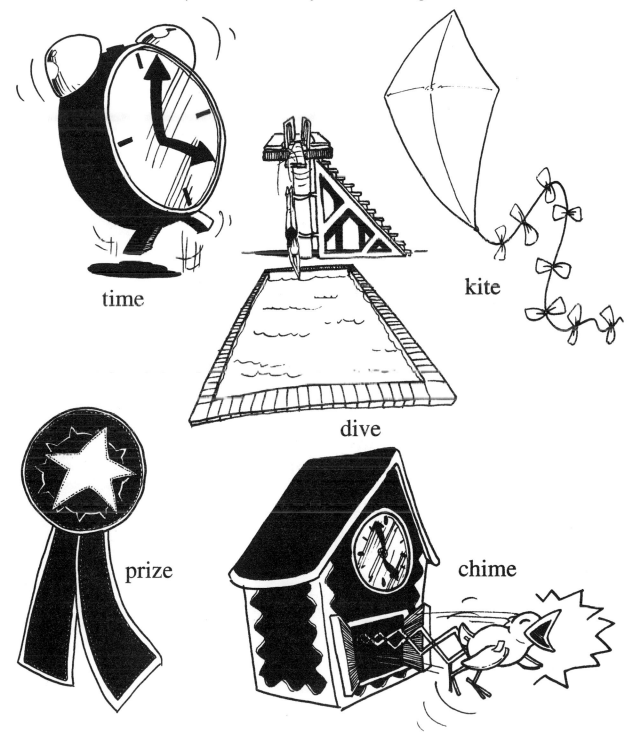

time

kite

dive

prize

chime

Read the words under the pictures. They all have the long "i" sound.

Can you choose the correct words?

1. Let me have a (bite mite) of your cake.

2. Kate lost her best (kite site) in the wind.

3. It is (lime time) to go back to the hall.

4. I think Dad drank a lot of (mine wine).

5. Put (five dive) stamps on this letter.

Great effort! Now see if you can write in the missing letters.

1. Let us go for a ride on our b _ kes.

2. A p _ le of plates fell off the counter.

3. The children did not dine till ni _ e.

4. You must not di _ e into that lake.

5. Will the crop get r _ pe in time?

My Score ⬚/10 That was excellent

Now choose the correct words.

1. Will the (pride bride) be late for her wedding?

2. Mum let my small brother go on the (slide glide).

3. Polish the silver cup and make it (shine chime).

4. This frog has (slime crime) on its back.

5. We (stile smile) if we have a lot of fun.

Good work!

Now choose the correct word from the list to complete the sentence.

List

1. It is a _____ to steal things.

ride

2. We shall go for a _____ if it is fine.

crime

3. The hall clock will _____ nine times.

twine

4. Sally got the same _____ as her mate.

chime

prize

5. Mike can fix the gate with thick _____ .

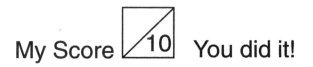 My Score ⬛/10 You did it!

Lesson 21

For the tutor

Read the words under the pictures below. They all have the long "o" sound.

drove

bone

broke

cone

stove

home

Now choose the correct words in brackets.

1. Jade gave her pup a big (bone tone).

2. We must be back (dome home) at five.

3. Your (hose nose) drips if you have a cold.

4. The girl (code rode) her bike to the shops.

5. Mum wants to plant a red (rose nose).

Terrific reading!
Add the missing letters to these words.

1. Our dog likes to d _ ze on a soft rug.

2. Mend the h _ se with this bit of twine.

3. Mike got a skipping ro _ e for a prize.

4. Do not p _ ke the cat with a stick.

5. I h _ pe the clock can still chime.

My Score ⬜/10 Well done!

See if you can choose the correct words.

1. Dad (grove drove) us to the lake at dinner time.

2. Jane (chose close) a silver cup as a prize.

3. Will the bus stall on this (slope scope)?

4. Take the plastic plate off the hot (stove trove).

5. Do not let the pup (broke choke) on its bone.

Well done!

Fill in the gaps with a word from the list.

List

1. A small girl _____ her leg on the slide.

close

2. _____ the gate as you go.

stone

3. Bike _____ can rust if they get wet.

spokes

4. The king sits on a golden _____ .

broke

5. Our home is made of _____ and bricks.

throne

My Score ⬜/10 Way to go!

Lesson 22

"u"-consonant-"e" (long "u")

For the tutor

"u"-consonant-"e" is a bit tricky. It can have two sounds: the name of the letter (long "u"), and "oo" as in "moo". The pictures below show what I mean. The letter "a" at the start or end of a word can have a short "u" sound as in "bun". Can you see an example?

amuse

jukebox

rule

salute

tune

Now choose the correct words.

1. My mother has to (use fuse) an old stove.

2. (Rule Mule) your lines with this red pen.

3. Miff is such a (mute cute) pup.

4. Bad (fumes fuses) came from the crane.

5. Dad broke the (amuse juke) box with his fist.

Use words from the list to fill in the gaps below.

List

1. Our camp is close to the sand _____ .

   dunes

2. A _____ is the same shape as a box.

   mules

3. Jake was warned not to be _____ to
   his teacher.

   tunes

   cube

4. Some _____ will not do as they are told.

   rude

5. The bride chose the _____ for her wedding.

My Score ⟋10 That was great!

Here are some more words using "u" - consonant - silent "e". Complete the sentences below.

List

1. Ken is _____ to the kids in his grade.

rude

2. Steve will _____ himself on the swings.

prune

Luke

3. Mum can _____ the roses with clippers.

fluke

4. It will be a _____ if we win a prize.

amuse

5. _____ pokes the frog with his finger.

You are improving all the time. Can you fill in the missing letters? (*You may need to explain the term "brute"*).

1. A rubber tube has a number of us _ s.

2. That br _ te hit the small pup with a stick.

3. All men must sal _ te the king on his throne.

4. Can you give us a tune on your f _ ute?

5. Sometimes Dad fl _ kes a win at golf.

My Score ⊿/10 Congratulations on a terrific effort!

Fish Game 4

- Photocopy and cut into squares. The aim is to show how vowel sounds are made long by adding "e".
- Deal out 6 cards each. Put the remaining cards in a pile between players.
- Have the first go to model the procedure.
- Example: "I have "win", do you have the word "wine"?" A correct match earns another turn and returns the matching pair to the pile. An incorrect match loses a turn.
- The player to lose all their cards first, wins.

wine	win	cute	cut
cub	cube	tub	tube
pine	pin	hop	hope
mate	mat	fat	fate
kite	kit	can	cane
sit	site	mad	made

First Aid for Reading © 1999. Permission for purchaser to copy for non-commercial classroom use. Pembroke Publishers

Lesson 23

For the tutor

You have already read examples of words ending with "s" and "es". There are many other ways of building on base words.

Look carefully at the sets of words below. Two words have lost the letter "e". Can you work out the rule for adding "ing" by yourself? (Clue: check the vowel sounds.)

ride	rider	riding
bake	baker	baking
dig	digger	digging

Fantastic! Now try these sentences for me.

1. A small pup is (choke choking) on its bone.

2. The crane (driving driver) just lost his job.

3. Two girls are (skipper skipping) up the slope.

4. Is Mum (maker making) cakes for the party?

5. Horses are (jumping jumps) over the barn fence.

My Score [/5] You did it!

Another way to build on a base word is to add the letter "n".

Josh *broke* a plate.

The plate is *broken*.

You can compare two things by adding "er" to the base word.

cute

cuter

My kitten is *cute*, but Dan's kitten is *cuter*.

To compare three or more things, add "est" to the base word.

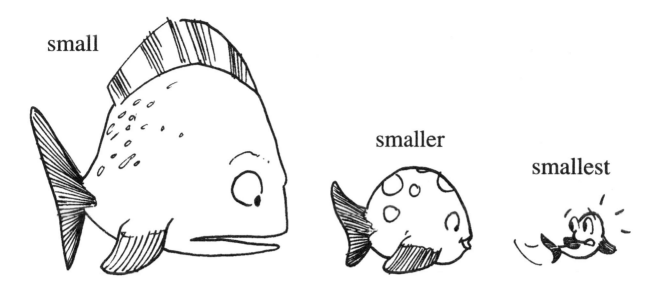

small

smaller

smallest

Try these sentences for me now.

1. Matt has (take taken) his dog for a run.

2. Shane has the (cute cutest) kitten of them all.

3. This dog has (blackest blacker) fur than that one.

4. My brother is much (braver bravest) than I am.

5. Have you (spoke spoken) to the bus driver yet?

My Score  / 5 What a star!

Lesson 24

For the tutor

Today's sight words are "water" and "please". Did you know the letter "c" can make the same sound as the letter "s"?

Read the words under the pictures to see what I mean.

slice

mice

price

dance

dice

race

Great! Now try the sentences below. Sound out any words you don't know, for example, t-i-ck-e-t, tick-et.

1. All (dice mice) have six sides.

2. Wash the mud from your (lace face).

3. Put (ice nice) cubes in the water jug.

4. Can we make (lice rice) for our lunch?

5. My sister will win the next (race pace).

That's right. Now add the missing letters if you can. (You may need to explain the meaning of "wince").

1. Lan _ e has left his flute on the bus.

2. Is that a robin on the stone fe _ ce?

3. Please bake some cakes for the d _ nce.

4. Dad is a dun _ e at the game of golf.

5. You win _ e if you bang your finger.

My Score ⟋10 Congratulations on a fine effort

Here are some more examples of words using "ce" to make the sound "s". Can you choose the correct word in brackets?

1. Please give me a small (slice twice) of ham.

2. Salute the (since prince) as he drives by.

3. Take your (stance prance) for the next race.

4. My brother went to (France dance) by plane.

5. Can you tell me the (trice price) of this ticket?

Way to go! Now complete the sentences by adding the missing letters. You should read the whole sentence first to find meaning clues.

1. Shane had to ring the bell tw _ ce.

2. Our cat had a cha _ ce to get the mice.

3. Tell Bru _ e to stack the crates on the fence.

4. Tra _ e all these lines with a black pen.

5. The pr _ nce hit six golf balls in the water.

My Score ◻/10 You are making excellent progress!

Revision Lessons 19-24

• Join up the words that rhyme.

wince	leans
face	beaker
beans	breed
week	file
whip	heaps
leaps	mince
greed	chance
weaker	lace
lance	ship
while	peek

• *Write captions under the pictures.*

steals   ice-cream
dancers   whale

101

Lesson 25

For the tutor

Today's sight words are "could", "would", and "should". The lesson is about words using "wh" to make the sound "w".

whip

whiff

whack

why

whiskers

Try the sentences below. (*You may need to model how to sound out words, for example, L-a-n-c-e, L-an-ce*).

1. Could I crack this (whip whiz) please?

2. Lance gave his bad dog a (what whack).

3. (When Where) should they get back home?

4. Take a (whiff whiz) of those fumes.

5. (Which When) plate will I use for the rice?

That was great! Now choose one of the list words for each space. The sentence must make sense.

List

1. _____ did you put the spice rack?   why

2. _____ is the bus late?   whip

where

3. Mum can _____ up some cakes.

what

4. The brute _____ his pups on the face.   whacks

5. _____ chance would we have to win a prize?

My Score ⧄/10 Wonderful

Here are some more ways of using the sound "wh". Try to finish these sentences.
Remember, they must make sense. (*You may need to explain what a whippet is.*)

1. The (whippet whimper) is hunting for mice.

2. Could I have a (whale white) rabbit for a pet?

3. (Why What) was the stockman cracking his whip?

4. Mother is (whacking whisking) six egg whites.

5. Our kitten has fine black (whiskers whispers).

Very good reading! Can you add the missing letters for me? You need to read to the
end of the sentence to find meaning clues.

1. A dunce would drink w _ ile he drives.

2. Wh _ les swim in salt water, not fresh.

3. My place has a whi _ e stone fence.

4. Our dog whimpe _ s when it wants water.

5. Sometimes it is rude to wh _ sper.

My Score ⬜/10 I am really proud of you!

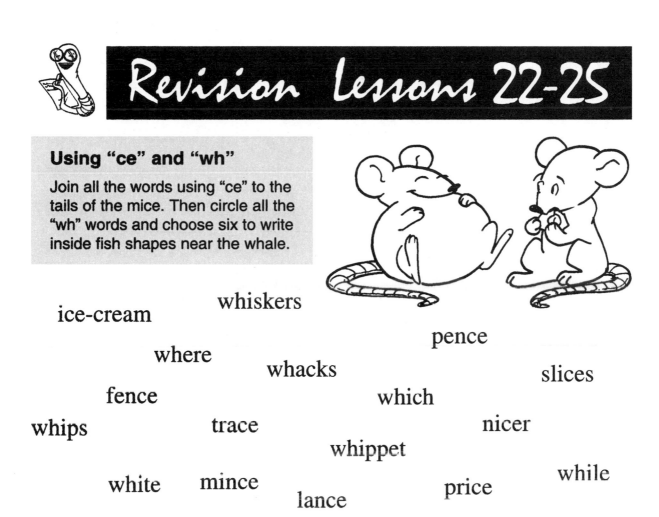

Using "ce" and "wh"

Join all the words using "ce" to the tails of the mice. Then circle all the "wh" words and choose six to write inside fish shapes near the whale.

ice-cream
whiskers
pence
where
whacks
slices
fence
which
whips
trace
nicer
whippet
white
mince
price
while
lance
rice
lace

Lesson 26

For the tutor

You can make the long "e" sound by adding an "e" to a word with a vowel and consonant: ("pet" becomes "Pete"). Another way is to use a double "e".

Read the picture words.

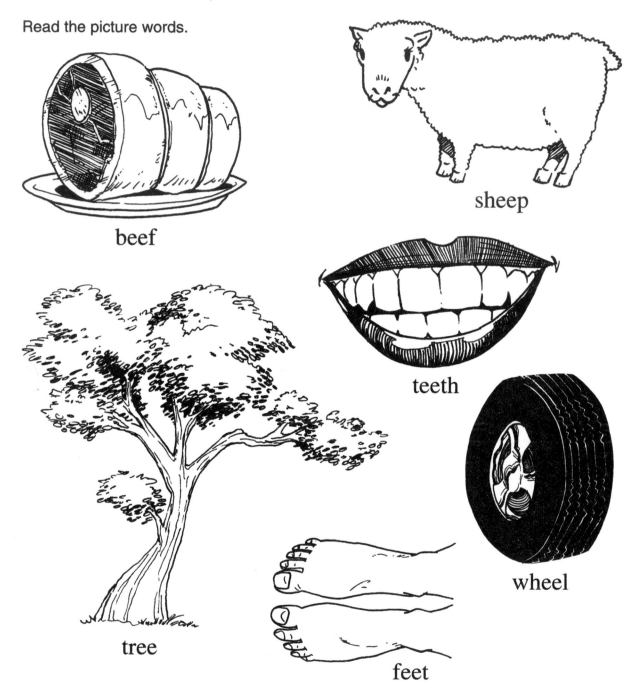

beef

sheep

teeth

tree

wheel

feet

Double "e" always has the same sound, which makes it quite easy to remember. Today's sight word is "said" (point). It is a very important word to remember.

See if you can choose the correct words in brackets. Sound out any words you are not sure of.

1. (Sees Bees) are buzzing in the hive.

2. Whales swim in (deep keep) water.

3. Can you (see fee) the missing crates?

4. We could all (feet meet) at the races.

5. This place (reeks seeks) of gas fumes.

Well done! Now choose a list word to complete the sentence.

List

1. Why do your _____ smell so much?

needs

2. When can we have _____ for dinner?

reef

seen

3. The whippet has _____ some mice.

feet

4. Mum said she _____ some help.

beef

5. Many fish swim in the coral _____.

That was easy for you!

My Score ⬛/10 Terrific reading!

Now you should be able to read some more difficult words using double "e". Complete the sentences below.

1. Which (free tree) will Dad need to prune?

2. Brush your (teeth wheel) well after dinner.

3. A fox (cheeps creeps) up to the chicken pen.

4. Nan went to (sleep sheep) at the meeting.

5. Steve made a frame with (steel heel) tubes.

You did it! Now add the missing letters. Remember to read the whole sentence first to find meaning clues.

1. Where is the back wh _ el of the bike?

2. When sle _ t falls, we get cold and wet.

3. Bruce likes white s _ eets on his bed.

4. The water is d _ eper on this side of the pond.

5. Could I have a slice of coff _ e cake please?

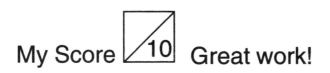

My Score ⟋10 Great work!

Lesson 27

For the tutor

Here is another way to make the long "e" sound: use "e" and "a" together. In most words with a blend of vowels, the first one can be heard, the second one is silent.

Read the words below for me.

teacher

beast

heat

beak

beach

read

Great! Now choose the word that fits best. (*You may need to model how to sound out words, for example, p-e-l-i-c-a-n, pel-ic-an: p-elican*).

1. My brother was in the winning (seam team).

2. Sweep all the (tea pea) pods into a heap.

3. Do you think I can (read bead) better?

4. (Heat Neat) three eggs in this small pan.

5. A brave man has no (tears fears).

Very good. Now choose a list word to complete the sentence.

List

lean

jeans

peas

beak

leaks

1. Water _____ from the old tap.

2. The pelican has a fish in its _____ .

3. Sweet _____ wilt in the heat.

4. Which _____ do you like best?

5. _____ the wheel on the tree trunk.

My Score ◻/10 You are doing really well. Keep it up!

There are lots of words using "ea" to make a long "e". Complete these sentences for me.

1. Do you (dream steam) while you sleep?

2. Lee could not (teach reach) the top shelf.

3. You need (beast yeast) to make bread.

4. Dean rides his bike to the (beach peach).

5. Have some (dream cream) with your coffee.

Amazing! Now I want you to add the missing letters. You will need to read the whole sentence to find meaning clues.

1. Place the te _ pot on the side counter.

2. A cunning fox sn _ aks up to the sheep.

3. Why are the peaches so che _ p?

4. What is the price of these j _ ans?

5. My teac _ er gave me a treat for a prize.

My Score ⟋10 Great reading!

The Bike Race

Dean's mother has given him a brand new ten speed bike for a birthday present. He decides to have a race along the street with his mates, Vince and Steve.

Just as Dean reaches top speed, the back wheel of his bike comes off and he smashes into the cream wooden fence belonging to his mean teacher, Mr Prince.

The bike is broken, and so is the fence! Dean does not want to take a chance. He sneaks off with his mates and hides the bike in a safe place until he has time to mend it.

Fish Game 5

- Photocopy and cut into squares. The aim is to find rhyming pairs.
- Deal out 6 cards each. Put the remaining cards in a pile between players.
- Have the first go to model the procedure.
- Example: "I have mice, do you have the word that rhymes?" A correct match earns another turn and returns the matching pair to the pile. An incorrect match loses a turn.
- The player to lose all their cards first, wins.

mice	nice	dance	lance
whale	pale	coffee	toffee
tree	free	where	there
disk	whisk	sweeping	sleeping
teach	reach	reader	leader
prince	mince	price	twice

Lesson 28

For the tutor

You already know how to make a long "a" using vowel, consonant, and "e", as in "came". The same sound can also be made with the letters "a" and "y" together.

Read the examples below. Today's sight word is "who".

crayfish

play

paying

holiday

Can you choose the words that fit best? (*You may need to model how to sound out words, for example, t-ea-ch-ing*).

1. What did the teacher (say bay) to you?

2. The sun's (rays ways) give us heat.

3. Many horses need (pay hay) in summer.

4. We spent the (day lay) picking peaches.

5. Who can (clay play) a tune on this flute?

Way to go! Now use the list words to complete the sentences.

List

1. Put the coffee mugs on the green _____ .

   tray

2. Our team plays _____ next week.

   slay

3. These nice pots are made of _____ .

   away

4. Did you _____ much for that ice-cream?

   clay

5. I hope the prince can _____ the beast.

   pay

My Score ⧄/10 Great!

Here are some more words using "ay". Can you choose the words that fit best?

1. Who is (praying playing) in our team today?

2. (Spray Bray) some water on the wilting roses.

3. The sheep could (stray tray) from the fence.

4. We may pick apples on (holiday Sunday).

5. Do you like eating (silverfish crayfish)?

Correct. Now add the missing letters to make "ay" words. Don't forget to read the whole sentence first.

1. Did you see the displ _ y of cream cakes?

2. Lance went diving for fish yester _ ay.

3. The pla _ ful pup is chasing the small kitten.

4. Dad is teaching me to play golf on S _ nday.

5. Water is spr _ ying from the leaking pipe.

My Score ⧄/10 You are doing really well!

 *Lesson 29*

For the tutor
Here is another way to make the long "a" sound. The sight words are "because" and "does"
(point). Read the picture words first.

train

snail

sail

rain

Here are some sentences to complete. (*You may need to model how to sound out*
words, for example, y-e-s-t-e-r-d-a-y, y-es-ter-day.)

1. Small brothers can be a real (gain pain).

2. Some boys like to play in the (rain main).

3. Our hens (paid laid) seven white eggs today.

4. Bang in this (nail pail) with the hammer.

5. Does your ship (fail sail) next Sunday?

Well done. Now use the list words to complete the sentences.

List

1. Did any _____ come yesterday?

2. Stay inside because it may _____ later.

3. Steve _____ a visit to his older brother.

4. Our pup wags its _____ to greet us.

5. Where did the fisherman get his _____ ?

tail

paid

bait

mail

rain

My Score ⟋10⟍ Good work!

The letters "ai" nearly always make a long "a" sound. Try these sentences for me now.

1. The bride chose a (slain plain) wedding dress.

2. Why did the (train grain) come off the rails?

3. (Paint Faint) the gate while the sun is shining.

4. Children should not play in the deep (drain brain).

5. The (frail trail) ends near the side of the lake.

Very good. Now use the list words to complete the sentences. Remember, they must make sense.

List

1. Do not _____ your back lifting crates.

2. Does the _____ have any crayfish?

3. Why are you _____ of thunder?

4. The sink is made of _____ steel.

5. _____ have eaten all our seedlings.

waiter

snails

stainless

afraid

strain

Can you find the letter "a" which makes a short "u" sound as in "bun"?

My Score ⟋10⟍ Excellent!

Story Lessons 1-29

The Pain

Gail asked if she could meet three friends at the boat races.

"Yes, but you will have to take Joe. I need to set up a display at the hall," said her mother.

Gail was not pleased. "Joe is such a pain!" she moaned.

"Stay at home, then," snapped her mother.

Gail grabbed Joe's hand and dragged him to the bay. Her friends were waiting near the fountain.

"Stay here and count the boats," Gail told Joe. "We want to buy some ice-cream."

But Joe was soon tired of counting and strayed away. Much later, when they finally found him, he was fast asleep on the beach. Meanwhile, Gail and her friends had missed all the races. They were not impressed.

Revision Lessons 28-29

Using "ay" and "ai"

Join all the "ai" words to the toy train. Then draw six (6) haystacks like the one in the picture. Choose six (6) "ay" words and write them inside your haystacks.

raining

frays

today

clay   train

holiday

grain

crayfish

Sunday

waiting   pains

afraid

may   stray

plays   faint

Lesson 30

For the tutor

The letters "oa" and "oe" usually make a long "o" sound. Read the words under the pictures to see what I mean.

foam

toast

boat

float

Good. Now choose the word that fits best and circle it. (*You may need to model how to sound out words, for example, m-a-tt-r-e-ss, m-at-tr-ess.*)

1. There are three green frogs in the (goat moat).

2. Paul fell off the fence and broke three (toes hoes).

3. Please help your father (toad load) the trailer.

4. I like a soft (foam loam) mattress on my bed.

5. She was cold because she left her (boat coat) at home.

I like the way you are sounding out the hard words. Now choose a list word to complete the sentences.

List

1. Seals are asleep on top of the ice _____ .

    goes

2. Some _____ are a real pest in the crops.

    moan

3. Why does that brat _____ all the time?

    toads

4. Peter _____ to hockey practice on Sundays.

    soap

5. Use this _____ to wash the dishes.

    floe

My Score ⟋10 You are doing very well!

Here are some more interesting words using the sound "oa". See if you can complete these sentences correctly.

1. Does the (poach coach) make you train each day?

2. We must wait until the (toast coast) is clear.

3. Steel pipes cannot (float bloat) in water.

4. Toads are (croaking groaning) in the moat.

5. Shane put a crumpet in the (toaster coaster).

Good reading! Now add the missing words for me please.

List

1. Jay has a bone stuck in his _____ .

    cloak

2. The _____ hid his traps in a drain.

    roast

3. Should we steam the duck or _____ it?

    poacher

4. Jean has an ink stain on her best _____ .

    floating

5. Many boats are _____ in the bay.

    throat

My Score ⟋10 That was excellent!

Fish Game 6

- Photocopy and cut into squares. The aim is to find rhyming pairs.
- Deal out 6 cards each. Put the remaining cards in a pile between players.
- Have the first go to model the procedure.
- Example: "I have mice, do you have the word that rhymes?" A correct match earns another turn and returns the matching pair to the pile. An incorrect match loses a turn.
- The player to lose all their cards first, wins.

cray	tray	sprayed	strayed
goes	foes	boat	coat
pouch	crouch	kissed	hissed
spout	scout	mountains	fountains
floating	bloating	poached	coached
painting	fainting	train	grain

Lesson 31

For the tutor

This lesson is about the letters "ou", which usually make the sound "ow", as in cow. Read the picture words first to see some familiar examples.

loud

count

clouds

out

Good! Now choose the word in brackets that fits best. Make sure the sentence makes sense.

1. Three men came (out pout) of the boat cabin.

2. Did you hear a (loud lout) bang yesterday?

3. Joan has eaten that bunch of (our sour) grapes.

4. The fat pig poked its (stout snout) in the drain.

5. Several girls are sitting on the (pouch couch).

Well done! Now read the list of words and work out where to write them.

List

1. Fay can _____ to one hundred.

2. This green teapot has a long _____ .

3. Dan is going _____ fishing in the stream.

4. Our teacher told us _____ cane toads.

5. Do not make a _____ while your sister is asleep.

List

about

trout

sound

count

spout

My Score [/10] That was terrific reading!

Here are some useful hints to help you tackle unfamiliar words by yourself:
- Sound out the word if you can (for example, sh-out-ing).
- Look for small words inside long ones (for example, "rain" in "straining").
- Read to the end of the sentence to find meaning clues.
Remember, the sentence must make sense.

1. Those black (snouts clouds) could bring rain.

2. Jean (sounds bounds) as if she is cross.

3. Why was Dad (shouting spouting) at you?

4. My sister likes to eat green (sprouts scouts).

5. Dogs are splashing in the (mountain fountain).

Great! Now let's do something different. The words in the sentences below have been mixed up. Try to unscramble them. To help you, each first word has a capital letter.

1. coffee nice ground is This.

2. sailing boats south are Seven.

3. sticks mush The in pig its the snout.

4. can a children Some count thousand to.

5. up They the trail mountain bikes on rode.

My Score [/10] Congratulations! That was just brilliant!

• Join up the words below that rhyme.

prayed	pounce
bounce	slaying
brain	spout
toad	roasted
snout	paint
found	grain
coat	strayed
boasted	sound
faint	road
playing	moat

Using "oa" and "ou"

Write the "oa" words under the boat.
Write the "ou" words under the cloud.

mouth

snout

toad

groan

float

our   coach

boast

sound   counting

coast

about

Lesson 32

Using "ed"
sight words: their people

For the tutor

Did you know that the past tense ending "ed" has two different sounds? Read the picture words to see what I mean.

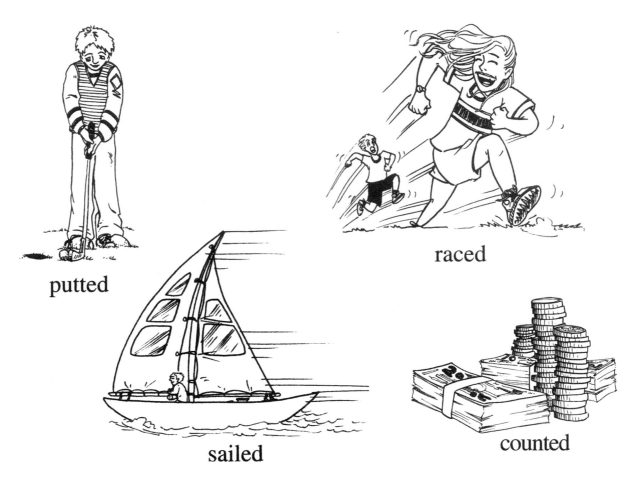

putted

raced

sailed

counted

The sight words are "their" (meaning belonging to them) and "people". Choose the word in brackets that fits best. Make sure the sentence makes sense.

1. People (filled killed) their plates with roast beef.

2. Who would like some (banned canned) peaches?

3. Shane (putted butted) his golf ball off the green.

4. A number of boats (failed sailed) into the bay.

5. The two girls (laced raced) each other home.

Good. Now write in the word that fits best in the space provided.

List

1. Do you still save _____ stamps?

2. We were _____ of playing tennis.

3. Have the letters been _____ yet?

4. My brother was _____ inside a mine.

5. James _____ his mother when he left home.

List
tired
kissed
trapped
mailed
used

My Score ⬜/10 Way to go!

Now for some more challenging words. If you have problems, remember to look for what you know. Choose the word in brackets that fits best.

1. A small boy (slipped flipped) on the wet ground.

2. They (tracked cracked) the nuts with their teeth.

3. Our cat (chased traced) the mice under a bench.

4. Grace (groaned gloated) because she had a pain.

5. Who wants (dreamed steamed) rice with chicken?

Well done. Lastly, write in the missing letters. You will need to read the whole sentence for meaning clues.

1. Some goats stray _ d away from the farm.

2. Bank tellers co _ nted up all the cash in the tills.

3. Fallen leaves flo _ ted on top of the water.

4. People scream _ d when their bus crashed.

5. I fell off the fence and sprai _ ed my left leg.

My Score ⬜/10 That was excellent reading!

Apple Pie

Paul felt foolish as he stood in front of his Grade 6 class. He had to explain how to bake an apple pie for a project.

"First of all, you need about five green cooking apples," he began. "You cut them into slices and place them in a saucepan. Mine are cooking over there on the stove now."

Paul paused. Dense black smoke was starting to billow from the saucepan. His fellow students tried hard not to laugh.

"Next, you need some pastry," he said, showing everyone what he had made the day before. The pastry looked awful. It was grey and lumpy.

"Then you put it in the pie dish," he continued. He picked up the pastry with grubby fingers and pressed it into shape.

"Lastly, add the cooked apples and bake." Paul scraped blackened apple pulp from the base of the saucepan.

"Anyone for apple pie?" asked the class clown.

Lesson 33

Using "-y", "-ey" (long "e") sight words: police woman women

For the tutor

The letter "y" can make a long "e" sound at the end of a word. Sometimes an "e" is needed as well, as in "donkey".

Read the picture words.

mice scurry

puppy

yummy

skippy

Today's sight words are "police", "woman", and "women". (Point out how the apostrophe is used in "brother's" to show who the piggy bank <u>belongs</u> to). Choose the word in brackets that makes more sense.

1. Sally raided her brother's (piggy jelly) bank.

2. Cathy sat on the couch and sucked a (dolly lolly).

3. Take that (dusty rusty) bike to the garbage dump.

4. Granny will be (sixty sixteen) on Sunday.

5. We sailed around the coast on a (berry ferry).

Great! Now read the words in the list and write them in the correct spaces.

List

1. A brave _____ chased the bank robber.

2. The boys were _____ for being cheeky.

3. Can we help _____ the cans of paint?

4. Jenny made a _____ coffee cake today.

5. Why were the police in such a _____ ?

hurry

woman

yummy

sorry

carry

My Score ⬜/10 Well done! That wasn't hard, was it?

Here are some more words using "y" and "ey". The letter "s" can be added to words ending in "ey". Look back at the pictures on page 129 to find out what happens to words ending with "y". Once again, work out which word in brackets fits best.

1. This (sloppy floppy) disk seems to be broken.

2. Mum put a (safety sticky) pin in the diaper.

3. Tammy dropped her (keys donkeys) in the moat.

4. (Twenty Plenty) of children are afraid of mice.

5. Give the (puppies poppies) small chunks of meat.

Well done! Now add the missing letters. You will need to read the whole sentence to find meaning clues.

1. Harry has three fl _ ffy white rabbits in his shed.

2. Rats sc _ rry about under the shop counter.

3. Stack these canned peaches on the p _ ntry shelf.

4. Molly is playing sk _ ppy with her small sisters.

5. There has been another rob _ ery at the bank.

My Score ⬜/10 *Great! You are making excellent progress!*

Lesson 34

For the tutor

Today's lesson is about words using the letters "ar", which usually make the sound "ar" as in car. Look at the pictures for more examples.

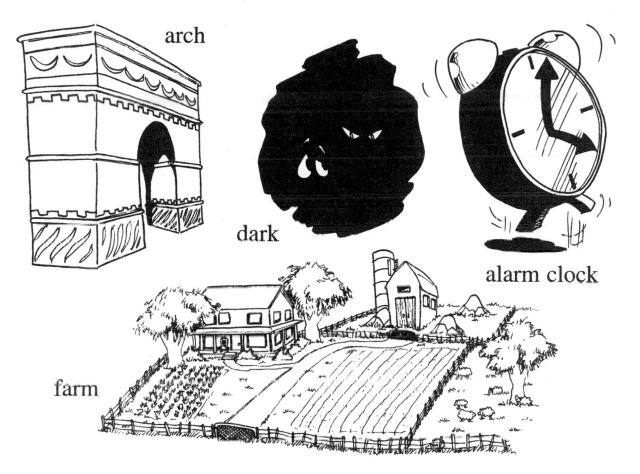

arch

dark

alarm clock

farm

The sight words you need to know are "office" and "busy". Now circle the words in brackets that make more sense.

1. Some children go to bed when it gets (lark dark).

2. The farmer carries hay into the (barn darn).

3. Dad always (parks marks) the car near his office.

4. Our dog (larks barks) loudly, but it does not bite.

5. A bus crashed into the side of the (march arch).

Good work! Read the list of words and write in the one that fits best in the space provided.

1. Thunder and rain will not _____ you.

2. Kerry was very _____ stocking the pantry.

3. My mother made a berry _____ for tea.

4. Our teacher helped us do the _____ sums.

5. I will not play _____ with you if you cheat.

My Score ⊿10 Excellent reading!

Here are some more challenging words for you. Read the sentences and choose the correct word in brackets.

1. Bobby is invited to our next (party smarty).

2. The driver could not (spark start) his bus today.

3. Silly girls think it is (smart scarf) to shoplift.

4. (Farmers Charmers) are busy planting wheat.

5. I lost my lucky (shark charm) in the playground.

Great! Now add the missing letters if you can. Read the whole sentence first to find meaning clues.

1. Everyone m _ rched as far as the crossroads.

2. The ga _ dener lost some seedlings in the frost.

3. Thousands of people attended m _ rket day.

4. Bart was al _ rmed when a donkey chased him.

5. Does your sister like going to kinderga _ ten?
Count the letters in the last word...wow!

My score ⊿10 You are making excellent progress!

 # Lesson 35

For the tutor

The letters "ow" can make different sounds. Today's lesson will cover words with the sound "ow" as in "cow". There are also examples of contractions (words joined together with an apostrophe). Look for others in later lessons.

Read the picture words for me. The sight word is "buy".

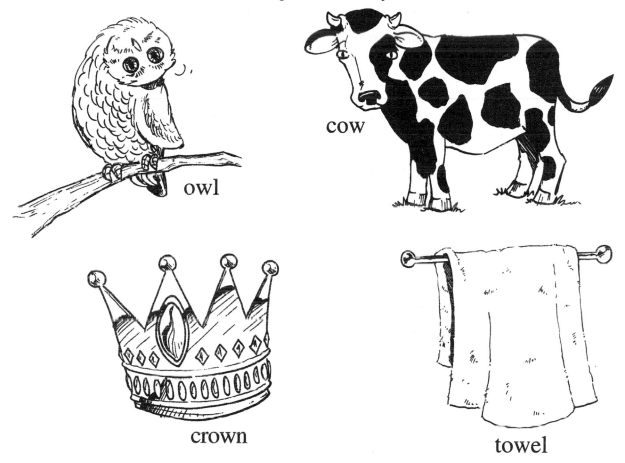

owl

cow

crown

towel

Read the sentences and circle the words in brackets that make sense.

1. Where did you (guy buy) those smart jeans?

2. Our (town down) is far away in the mountains.

3. The bride chose a lace wedding (gown down).

4. A black dog (owls howls) outside the farm gate.

5. Do not let the (cows bows) into the garden.

Way to go! Now read the list of words, then write the correct word in the space provided.

List

1. An old woman has fallen _____ the steps.

2. Dad hired a funny _____ for my party.

3. The teacher added another _____ to her chart.

4. He's playing in the barn with a _____ puppy.

5. _____ many candies can I buy with five dollars?

row

clown

how

brown

down

My Score ⟋10 Very good reading!

Here are some more complex words using the sound "ow". Complete the sentences in the same way as before.

1. The prince was (crowned frowned) on Sunday.

2. Let's pick a big bunch of (showers flowers).

3. People (crowded drowned) into the market.

4. Americans like eating clam (powder chowder).

5. A panther (clowned prowled) around the huts.

Now fill in the missing letters. You will need to read the whole sentence to find meaning clues.

1. Three women d _ owned at the beach yesterday.

2. My tummy is gro _ ling because I am hungry.

3. Use this fluffy t _ w _ l when you have a shower.

4. What's that brown po _ der on the pantry shelf?

5. The teacher f _ owned at me because I was late.

My score ⟋10 Fantastic!

Using "ar"

Circle the words that use the sound "ar". Say all the words.

arch
display
mound
throat
chart
cards
thrilled
shark
champ
darker

Draw an alarm clock.

Using "ow"

Circle the words that use the sound "ow". Say all the words.

plump
owls
clown
powder
crouch
groans
frowned
chase
chowder
fainting

Draw a crown.

Using "y" and "ey"

Write the correct word underneath each picture. Say all the words.

smelly

yummy

donkey

windy

For the tutor
This lesson will help you learn words using a silent "e".

Read the picture words.

shuttle   cheese

bottle   house

See if you can circle the words in brackets that fit best. The sentences must make sense.

1. A hungry cat creeps into the empty (mouse house).

2. Fill up this empty (bottle bubble) with coffee.

3. Put some (cheese breeze) in the trap for the mice.

4. My (little battle) sister starts kindergarten today.

5. Our kitten played in a (muddle puddle) of water.

Well done! Now read the words and complete the sentences.

List

1. That tabby cat will get angry if you _____ it.

2. Mr. Jones drove his _____ to the sale yards.

3. Our car stopped in the _____ of the road.

4. _____ the sprouts in plenty of fresh water.

5. A leaking _____ is really useless.

kettle

tease

rinse

cattle

middle

My score ◻/10 You are a star!

Here are more words using a final silent "e". You can circle the words in brackets that fit best.

1. Many people like to (paddle gamble) at the races.

2. Would you like a trip in a space (shuffle shuttle)?

3. The (candle handle) flickered before it went out.

4. Buy (twelve shelve) brown towels for presents.

5. Larry (stumbled mumbled) on the steep mountain path.

Way to go! Finally, add the missing letters. It is a good idea to read the whole sentence to find meaning clues.

List

1. I've spilt some grease on my best _____ .

2. Kerry likes to _____ up to her uncle.

3. You _____ when you have a bad cold.

4. Terry bent the _____ of his bike.

5. Mrs. Lane made an apple _____ .

crumble

snuggle

handlebars

blouse

sniffle

My score ◻/10 That was fantastic reading!

Lesson 37

For the tutor

This lesson shows how to read words using the sound "or". There are other letter combinations which make the same sound; you will learn them later in the program.

Read the picture words first.

fork

snorkel

horn

sports

Good. The sight words are "fast", "last", "past", and "pass". Read the sentences and choose the correct word in brackets.

1. Uncle Norm likes to eat cake with a (cork fork).

2. Do not drive so (fast past) round sharp corners.

3. Would you please pass me some roast (pork dork)?

4. At least twelve boats are docked at the (fort port).

5. Many roses have very sharp (thorns horns).

Well done! Now choose the words that make sense.

1. The rider has tumbled off her _____ .

2. Why do you tell such _____ jokes?

3. Our family went on a picnic _____ Sunday.

4. We could _____ the crates under the house.

5. These trousers are a little _____ for me.

My score /10

List

short

last

horse

corny

store

There are lots of interesting words using the sound "or". Add the missing letters. You may need to read the whole sentence first to find meaning clues.

1. Training for the athletic s _ orts starts shortly.

2. There are about twelve plants on our back p _ rch.

3. The shrubs on the co _ ner need to be pruned.

4. Danny and Len had the sniffles again this morni _ g.

5. The unlucky gambler lost a fort _ ne playing cards.

Terrific reading! This time, the words in the sentences have been jumbled. See if you can write them in the correct order below. To help you, the first word has a capital letter. Good luck!

1. needed is underwater for A swimming snorkel .

2. is train platform Our leaving the now .

3. clouds bring Those thunderstorms dark could .

4. my wish stop uncle snoring would I !

5. a children sand of out made fortress The .

My score /10 That was brilliant!

Fish Game 7

- Photocopy and cut into squares. The aim is to find rhyming pairs.
- Deal out 6 cards each. Put the remaining cards in a pile between players.
- Have the first go to model the procedure.
- Example: "I have mice, do you have the word that rhymes?" A correct match earns another turn and returns the matching pair to the pile. An incorrect match loses a turn.
- The player to lose all their cards first, wins.

flowers	showers	crown	drown
shuffles	snuffles	table	fable
corn	torn	farm	harm
torch	porch	motel	hotel
skippy	whippy	parched	marched
marry	carry	jockey	hockey

 *Lesson 38*

For the tutor

You have already learned there are many ways to make long vowel sounds. In this lesson you will find out some more. The sight word is "friend"; it is tricky because of the silent "i". Read the picture words for me. Explain that a "biro" is a type of ball point pen.

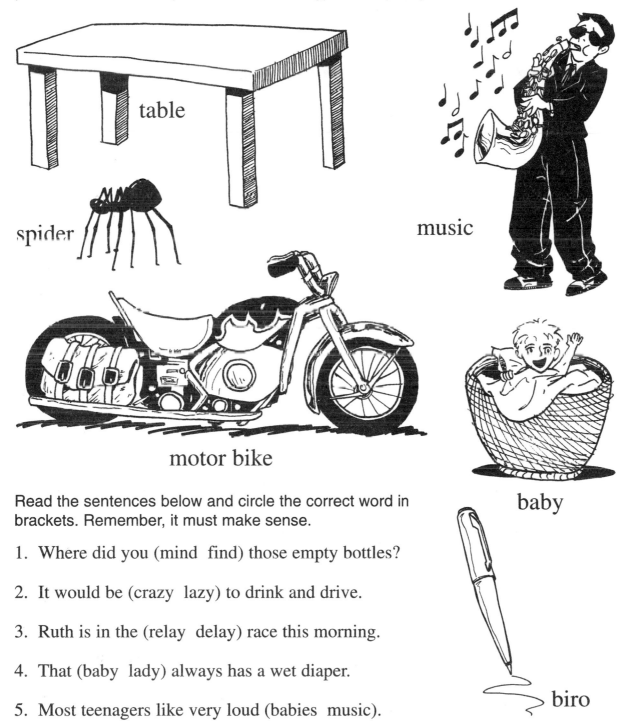

table

spider

music

motor bike

baby

biro

Read the sentences below and circle the correct word in brackets. Remember, it must make sense.

1. Where did you (mind find) those empty bottles?

2. It would be (crazy lazy) to drink and drive.

3. Ruth is in the (relay delay) race this morning.

4. That (baby lady) always has a wet diaper.

5. Most teenagers like very loud (babies music).

Great! Now read the list of words and write in the one that fits best.

1. What _____ of muffins do you prefer?

2. _____ coffee tables need to be painted.

3. Jade said _____ but we ignored her.

4 Our holidays start in the middle of _____ .

5. Tony collected the mail from the _____ office.

List

both

April

post

hello

kind

My score ⬜/10 Excellent reading!

If a word is unfamiliar, it sometimes helps to work out the sound of the vowel or vowels. A useful rule to remember is that words with a double consonant nearly always have a short vowel (for example, "slippers" and "running"). Words using "ck" and "sh" also have short vowels (for example, "sick" and "crash"). Read the sentences below and circle the correct word.

1. Place all the cards face down on the (fable table).

2. David is afraid of (spiders sliders) and earwigs.

3. The farmer shot a wild pig with his (trifle rifle).

4. Corey (grinds blinds) his teeth when he is angry.

5. Your plane (departs reports) in twenty minutes.

You are going really well. Now add the missing letters. It may help to read the whole sentence first to find meaning clues.

1. The hoste _ s offered her visitors some coffee.

2. My friends and I had a sup _ r time at the party.

3. You can buy cl _ thes at this department store.

4. Gr _ vy tastes nice with roast beef or chicken.

5. Two wild horses have escaped from the st _ bles.

My score ⬜/10 Wonderful!

Fish Game 8

- Photocopy and cut into squares. The aim is to find rhyming pairs.
- Deal out 6 cards each. Put the remaining cards in a pile between players.
- Have the first go to model the procedure.
- Example: "I have mice, do you have the word that rhymes?" A correct match earns another turn and returns the matching pair to the pile. An incorrect match loses a turn.
- The player to lose all their cards first, wins.

rake	make	cute	mute
bike	like	rope	hope
smoke	spoke	drive	five
tunes	dunes	stripes	pipes
bride	pride	grapes	drapes
trove	grove	brave	grave

Lesson 39

For the tutor

In some words, "on" sounds like "un". In others, the vowel is almost silent. Look at the picture words to see what I mean. The sight words today are "father" and "rather".

won

monkey

melon

season

Read the sentences and circle the word in brackets that fits the meaning.

1. Which team (son won) the soccer game last Friday?

2. Are there any ripe (felons melons) for dinner?

3. My father prefers (honey money) on his toast.

4. Lois is waiting at the (front fort) of the platform.

5. The greedy boy ate a (carton carbon) of ice-cream.

Very good! Now read the list and write in the missing words. You may need to read the whole sentence to find meaning clues.

List

1. Mum grated _____ rind for the apple tart.

2. Uncle Simon thinks both his _____ are lazy.

3. I _____ why the music has stopped?

4. My father has not _____ the shopping yet.

5. These slices of _____ seem rather salty.

sons

wonder

bacon

done

lemon

My score ☐/10 That was great!

Complete the sentences below in the usual way. Remember, they must make sense.

1. A (donkey monkey) is swinging from the branch.

2. Brian will visit his family in (London Monday).

3. I found the (button mutton) missing from my shorts.

4. July is in the middle of our summer (reason season).

5. Sharon won a (ribbon robin) in the final event.

Well done! Finally, add the missing letters. You may need to read to the end of the sentence to find meaning clues.

1. The greedy glut _ on gobbled up six bits of bacon.

2. A felon is a per _ on who has committed a crime.

3. Our trip to Florida last month was w _ nderful.

4. A cannonb _ ll was fired from the front of the fort.

5. Put more waterm _ lon slices on the empty platter.

My score ☐/10 Well done!

Lesson 40

For the tutor

Did you know that double "o" can make two quite different sounds? Read the picture words to see what I mean.

book

cool

cook

pool

Today's sight word is "platypus". See if you can circle the word in brackets that fits best.

1. Would you rather have a (moo cool) or a hot drink?

2. Sharon said she is able to (look cook) eggs and bacon.

3. The heated (pool tool) opens on Monday morning.

4. Red Riding (Hood good) picked flowers for Granny.

5. Hang your clothes on the (moon hook) over there.

Way to go! Now read the list of words and write in the one that fits best in the space provided.

List

1. My friend Jason has a rotten _____ .

   stood

2. Can you see the _____ on the top branch?

   tooth

3. The teacher _____ in front of the room.

   shook

4. We'll need a _____ to reach the top shelf.

   stool

5. Sandy _____ a dozen apricots off the tree.

   raccoon

My score ☐/10 Another fine effort! Keep it up.

Choose the correct word in brackets.

1. My little brother starts (spool school) on Monday.

2. Rifle (hooters shooters) are hunting in the forest.

3. The bride and (broom groom) are on honeymoon.

4. Some rotten (chooks crooks) stole all our money.

5. Leon's (balloon teaspoon) drifted into a puddle.

Good! Now try to add the missing letters. Don't forget to read the whole sentence to find meaning clues.

1. I wonder if these are m _ shrooms or toadstools?

2. Only Simon unders _ ood the reason for my anger.

3. Both kang _ roos have a tiny joey in their pouch.

4. We sto _ ped down to pick up a dozen lemons.

5. A plat _ pus is making its nest under the river bank.

My score ☐/10 Well done!

Using "on" and "oo"

Join all the "on" words to the branches and trunk of the lemon tree. Say all the words.

carton

cannon

monkeys

melon

wondering

money

reason

front

bacon

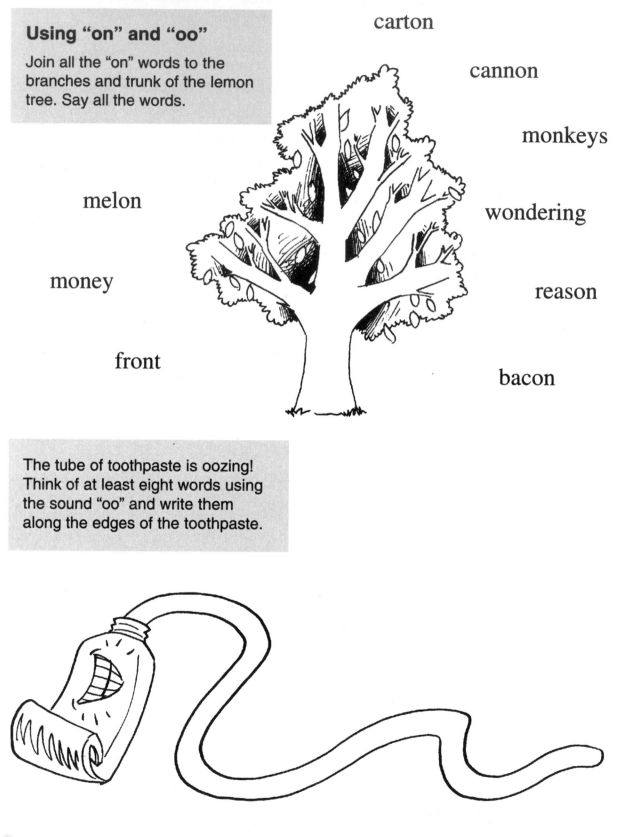

The tube of toothpaste is oozing! Think of at least eight words using the sound "oo" and write them along the edges of the toothpaste.

Lesson 41

For the tutor

The letters "ie" usually make a long "i" sound. The letter "y" at the end of a word can make either a long "e" as in "happy" or a long "i" as in "fly". In this lesson the new words have an "i" sound. Our sight word is "eye".

Read the picture words first.

pie

supply

apply

drying

flies

cloudy sky

Choose the word in brackets that fits best.

1. I wonder if a dragon (fly flies) breathes fire?

2. The (sky skies) is overcast, so it could soon rain.

3. (Pie Tie) up the present with this pink ribbon.

4. Judy (try tried) to read the book to her brother.

5. The baby (cry cried) because he had sore eyes.

cried

That was easy for you. Now read the list of words and fill in the gaps in the sentences.

List

1. I can _____ on my friends when I need help.

2. Soak the _____ mushrooms in cool water.

3. _____ have stolen secret plans from the safe.

4. The crooks _____ to police about the robbery.

5. A horse may _____ if it is startled by thunder.

dried

lied

shy

spies

rely

My score ⬜/10 Good work!

Did you notice that if you change base words ending in "y" (long "i") to make a plural or change the tense, the "y" is replaced with "ies" or "ied"? If not, check out the first exercise on the previous page. Now try to work out what the missing letters are and write them in. You may need to read the whole sentence to find meaning clues.

1. Our damp trousers are d _ ying on the clothes line.

2. The school has an ample su _ ply of pens and paper.

3. Your brother must app _ y for help at the front office.

4. Shannon's bedroom looked like a p _ gsty this morning.

5. Have you r _ plied to Uncle Simon's last letter yet?

Well done. Now let's see if you can unscramble the words to make sentences. To help you, the first words have capital letters. Write the sentences in the space below.

1. bacon wonderful That smells fried just.

2. flying is Craig next south Monday.

3. father job Is applying the for?

4. terrified that would crooks our were steal cash We.

5. our Mum buys supermarket in supplies the usually.

My score ⬜/10 You are a star!

Kelly's Cubby

Kelly's uncle built her a cubby for her ninth birthday. It was on a platform near the boundary fence, a long way from the main farm house.

Kelly invited twelve friends to a grand opening party. She hung paper streamers from the platform and spent a small fortune on nibbles and drinks.

The children played loud music and gobbled up all the food. They did not notice black storm clouds gathering outside. Soon the wind was howling and thunder crashing. Rain streamed down in torrents. Kelly and her friends huddled close together. It was really dark before they could be rescued by their worried fathers.

"How was your party?" Kelly's uncle asked several days later.

"Super," Kelly said with a sniffle, "apart from the storm!"

Lesson 42

For the tutor

The sound "or" can be made with "aw" and "au". When you see a word with "aw" in it, think of "saw". When you see "au", think of "sauce". The sight word today is "engine".

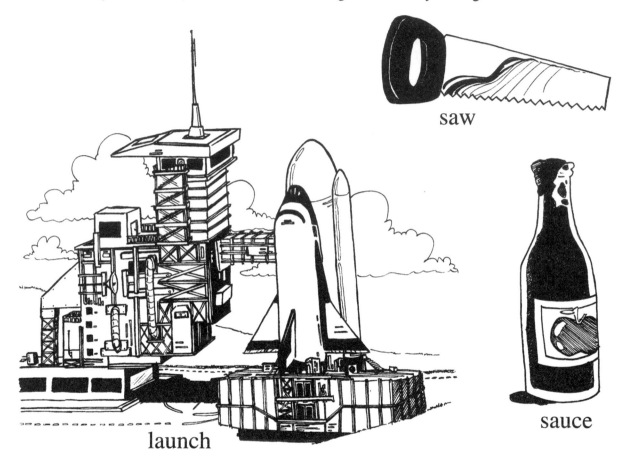

saw

sauce

launch

Read the sentences and choose the correct words in brackets. (You may need to explain the meaning of "flaws".)

1. Paul tried to trim the branch with a blunt (paw saw).

2. Do supermarkets supply (raw law) meat for animals?

3. The cloth used in cheap jeans may have (flaws claws).

4. Duck shooters usually start hunting at (lawn dawn).

5. Sally (pawns yawns) when she gets tired or bored.

paw

Great! Now read the list of words and fill in the spaces. You may need to read the whole sentence to find meaning clues.

List

1. Is there plenty of clean _____ in the stable?

2. Please pass the bottle of _____ for my ice-cream.

3. Use a cart to _____ the garbage away.

4. His motorbike _____ must be replaced soon.

5. Careless driving was the _____ of the smash.

haul

straw

cause

sauce

engine

My score ⬜/10 Excellent reading!

Here are some more difficult words using "aw" and "au". Read the sentences and choose the correct words in brackets.

1. My baby sister can (bawl crawl) from the kitchen to the family room.

2. Everyone said the spooky house was (haunted taunted).

3. The artist has (brawn drawn) some spotted toadstools.

4. Thousands of ants are (crawling brawling) everywhere.

5. Put those smelly clothes in the (launder laundry).

You are doing really well! Now add the missing letters. You may need to read the whole sentence to find meaning clues.

1. Most cooks prefer to use stainless steel s _ ucepans.

2. Our summer months are June, July and A _ gust.

3. This engine will soon need a complete overha _ l.

4. A spaceship was l _ unched last Friday morning.

5. The captain of the fishing tr _ wler drowned yesterday.

My score ⬜/10 You are doing really well!

Using "aw" and "au"

Draw pictures to match the words.

bawl

paw

dawn

saw

crawl

awful

Write the "au" words under the saucepans. Say all the words.

Paul   sauce   pause   haunted   laundry   August

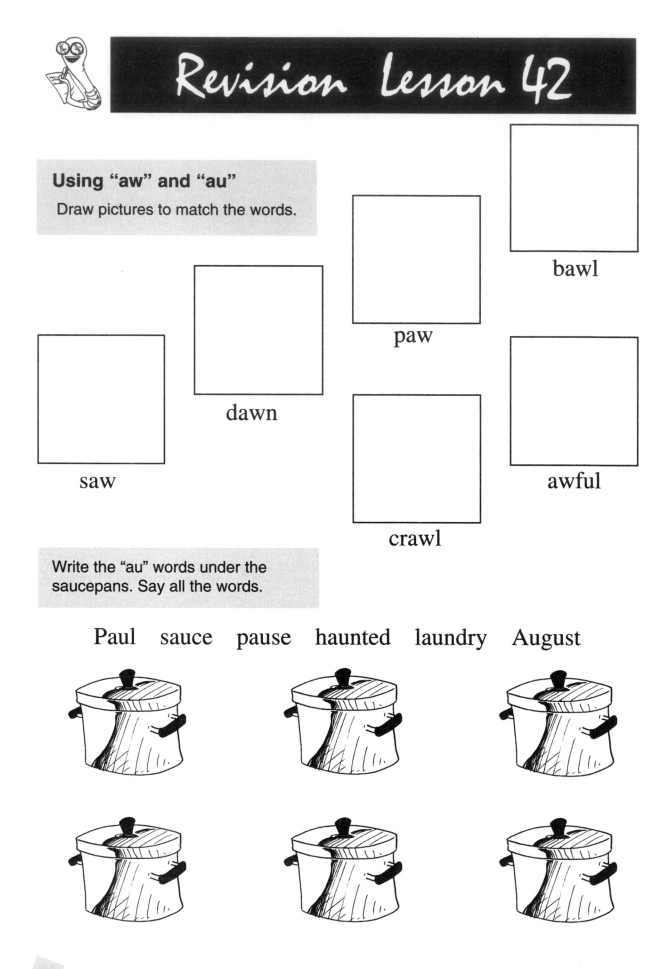

Lesson 43

Using "ow" (long "o")
sight word: weird

For the tutor

You have already learned the sound "ow" as in "cow". The same letters can also make a long "o" sound. Look at the pictures for examples. The sight word is "weird".

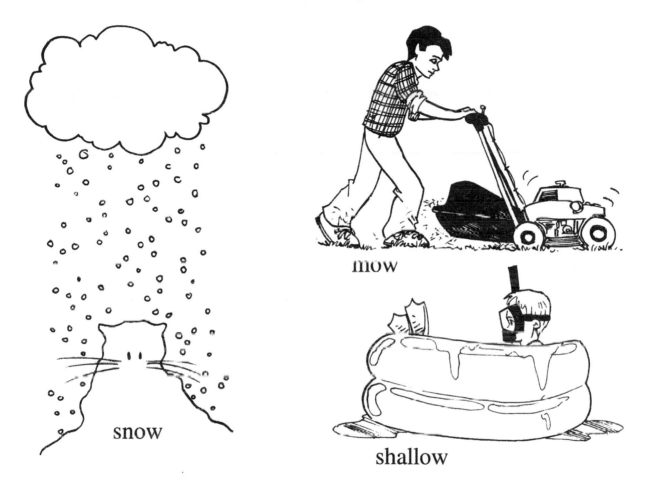

snow

mow

shallow

Now read the sentences and choose the correct words in brackets. The sight word is "weird".

1. Both boys refused to (tow mow) the front lawn.

2. Please (stow show) us how to start this engine.

3. If you (glow blow) your nose too hard, it could bleed.

4. Paula likes to paint (snowy slow) mountain slopes.

5. The farmer has (grown shown) a fine wheat crop.

crow

First Aid for Reading © 1999. Permission for purchaser to copy for non-commercial classroom use. Pembroke Publishers   155

Way to go! Read the words and write them in the correct space.

	List
1. _____ the muddy pants into the laundry basin.	slowed
2. The racing cars _____ down at the corners.	window
3. Open the _____ if the bedroom is stuffy.	narrow
4. A _____ path leads to the haunted house.	throw
5. Something _____ happened last August.	weird

My score ◻/10 Well done!

Here are some more challenging examples of words using "ow". See if you can add the missing letters. It is a good idea to read the whole sentence to look for meaning clues.

1. An angry teacher b _ llowed at the cheeky girls.

2. Toddlers paddled in the sh _ llow water of the lake.

3. The vet fed the baby s _ arrow with an eyedropper.

4. Children were throwing snowb _ lls at each other.

5. Our wheelbar _ ow is very rusty.

Great! Finally, try to unscramble the words to make sentences. To help you, the first words have capital letters. Write the sentences below.

1. snowman nose carrot a had Our cute.

2. trunk nesting Possums in hollow that are tree.

3. problems when burrows Rabbits they cause dig.

4. overflowed tank from last their Water year.

5. pink to Use decorate marshmallows trifle the.

My score ◻/10 Brilliant!

- Join up the words that rhyme.

hurry	parched
charmed	crumble
cable	sunny
marched	scored
frowning	scurry
grumble	finder
minder	most
snored	drowning
post	harmed
funny	fable

- Write captions under the pictures.

candles clothes

stormy trifle

Lesson 44

For the tutor
The letter combinations "oy" and "oi" make exactly the same sound. Try to think of "boy" or "oil"
when you see those letters in a word.

oil

boy

toy

boil

Read the sentences and decide which words in brackets fit best. The sight words are
"blood" and "flood".

1. Twenty (toys boys) went sailing on the motor launch.

2. (Soy Joy) sauce is nice on noodles and fried rice.

3. The wheels of my bike skidded in a pool of (oil foil).

4. Ask Dan to make coffee when the kettle (boils oinks).

5. We expect the river will (blood flood) again soon.

Good work! Now read the list of words and write in the one that fits best.

1. Take plenty of _____ to the laundromat.

2. Carrots and parsnips do not need rich _____ .

3. _____ made a wooden engine for the baby.

4. Tony is going to _____ the Scouts next month.

5. We hauled the _____ of plastic pipe in a wheelbarrow.

List:
coils
join
coins
Troy
soil

My score ☐/10   Great reading!

Read the sentences and decide which words in brackets fit best. Circle the correct answers.

1. Did everybody (annoy enjoy) the music at the dance?

2. A weird (poise noise) came from the narrow tunnel.

3. Paula is (loyal royal) to most of her friends at school.

4. Chocolate cake tastes nicest when it is (hoist moist).

5. It is very rude to (joint point) your finger at others.

Excellent! Now add the missing letters. Don't forget to read the whole sentence to find meaning clues.

1. Raw o _ sters and crayfish can make some people ill.

2. Sp _ ilt children are likely to cry for no reason at all.

3. Store bottles of po _ son out of reach of toddlers.

4. The menu offers a ch _ ice of roast chicken or beef.

5. Did the crooks destr _ y the evidence of their crime?

My score ☐/10   Super reading!

Using "oy" and "oi"

The "oy" and "oi" words are all mixed up.
Find the "oy" words first and circle them.
Then draw boxes around the "oi" words.

noise

boy   points

coy

soil   enjoyed

joyful

foil

Troy   coils

boiled   destroy

• Join up the words that rhyme.

mutton	cried
claws	button
fried	taunt
received	season
fellow	flaws
crows	deceived
jaunt	caused
paused	yellow
reason	groom
broom	grows

Lesson 45

For the tutor
The letter "g" can make the sound "j" when it is combined with an "e". Today's sight words are "machine" and "iron".

page

cage

fridge

large

Read the sentences and decide which words in brackets fit best. Circle the correct answers.

1. Carmel is paid a small (age wage) for babysitting.

2. A tiger has escaped from its (cage rage) at the zoo.

3. She lost a (huge rude) amount of blood in the accident.

4. I enjoyed the last (sage page) of the book best of all.

5. It took only a second to (irons iron) the yellow tie.

That was easy for you! Now read the list of words and decide which one fits best in the space provided.

List

1. _____ is sometimes used for seasoning.

2. Remember to oil that _____ monthly.

3. The hungry boy asked for a _____ meat pie.

4. A leaking pen spoiled the _____ of my page.

5. We applauded the actors as they left the _____ .

sage

edge

stage

machine

large

My score ⬚/10 Very good reading!

Many interesting words can be made using the letters "ge". Read the sentences and decide which words in brackets fit best. Circle the correct answers.

1. Dad replaced the rusty (binge hinge) on the gate.

2. I can make chocolate (budge fudge) without your help.

3. Floods swept the wooden (fridge bridge) downstream.

4. Seals and sea lions (plunged lunged) into the icy waters.

5. Never get in a car with a complete (ranger stranger).

Good work! Now add the missing letters. You may need to read the whole sentence to find meaning clues.

1. I was annoyed because Joy ch _ nged her mind twice.

2. Several teen _ gers were lost while on a camping trip.

3. Police have destroyed all the for _ ed bank notes.

4. That jacket with long frin _ es at the bottom looks cool.

5. Can we exc _ ange this video for another one please?

My score ⬚/10 Excellent!

Lesson 46

For the tutor

There are four ways of making the sound "er". The most common one uses "e" and "r", but you can use all the other vowels with "r" except "a". Look at the picture words first.

birthday

bird

furnace

church

fir tree

work

fur coat

burst

Read the sentences and decide which words in brackets fit best. Circle the correct answers.

1. Sally enjoyed stroking her kitten's soft (fir fur) coat.

2. Their old fridge no longer (works words) properly.

3. Two (birds burns) are nesting on my window ledge.

4. The toddler (furls curls) up on the couch to sleep.

5. (Dirt Hurt) and mud have soiled the carpet.

Good! Now read the list and decide where the words should go. Write them in.

List

1. The hedgehog was _____ in the bush fire.

2. Baby possums are cute, _____ animals.

3. Hunters _____ spears at the huge bear.

4. One _____ of the bank notes were forged.

5. Dad looks strange in his yellow, flowery _____ .

burned

hurled

third

shirt

furry

My score ☐/10 Terrific reading!

You are making excellent progress. Before you try the more difficult words on this page, which vowel **can't** be used to make the sound "er"? Good! Read the sentences and decide which words in brackets fit best. Circle the correct answers.

1. How much are those engines (worth   worst)?

2. The (churn   church) service starts at ten o'clock.

3. (Thirty   Thirsty) birds were released from the cage.

4. The wooden bridge (burst   burned) into flames.

5. David wanted a ham (murder   burger) for dinner.

Correct! Can you add the missing letters? You should read the whole sentence first to find meaning clues.

1. Workers stoked the f _ rnace with chopped wood.

2. Mum was bu _ sting with pride when I won the race.

3. My ninth birt _ day party is on Saturday afternoon.

4. Why did they spoil the fridge by painting it pu _ ple?

5. The m _ rderer was sentenced to life imprisonment.

My score ☐/10 You are a star!

The Banquet

Last Saturday, King Curly invited about thirty people to a banquet at the royal palace. His servants had worked for weeks till every surface glowed. Tables were covered with huge platters of fresh oysters, cheese, and other fine foods. Casks of wine lined the entrance hall.

The hungry guests arrived at the edge of the moat.

"Lower the drawbridge!" ordered King Curly.

Rusty chains clanked and hinges creaked as two strong servants turned the handles. Suddenly the chains, which had not been oiled for years, snapped. The heavy drawbridge crashed into the moat, squirting muddy water over the crowd. Women squealed with annoyance as their expensive gowns were soaked.

King Curly was furious.

"The royal banquet is cancelled!" he bellowed, and his disappointed guests returned to their homes.

• Join up the words that rhyme.

cause	sorrow
loyalty	hurting
felon	scooped
boiled	royalty
curling	paunch
forged	flirt
dirt	pause
launch	gorged
borrow	melon
stooped	soiled

• Write captions under the pictures.

clap
flying
cherry pie
strawberry

Lesson 47

For the tutor

The letter "q" is followed by a "u" and generally makes the sound "kw". The letter combination "ea" sometimes makes a long "a" sound, as in the sight words. What sound does it usually make? (Tutor: Write the word "eat" if necessary.)

squirts

quack

liquid

queen

Read the sentences and complete them in the usual way.

1. The (quits quins) were born on the first of August.

2. There is a choice of (stake steak) or trout for dinner.

3. Kirk had a (great grate) time throwing snowballs.

4. Dad (quiz quit) work because he burned both arms.

5. Be (quick quack) or we will have the worst seats.

Choose a list word to complete these sentences.

List

1. The wicked _____ was locked in a dungeon.

2. Mum let me choose my own _____ last year.

3. You look _____ without your front teeth.

4. The greedy man gobbled up a huge _____ .

5. Our carpet is _____ dirty around the edges.

quilt

queen

queer

steak

quite

My score ⬚/10 Wonderful!

That wasn't hard, was it? Now add the missing letters. You may need to read the whole sentence to find meaning clues.

1. Sq _ eeze oranges and lemons to make a cold drink.

2. Boiling water squ _ rted from the broken pipes.

3. Ice-cream turns into a liq _ id when it is melted.

4. Colin has been fined for bre _ king the speed limit.

5. Can you hear mice s _ ueaking between the walls?

Great!
This time I want you to unscramble the words to make sentences. Write them in the space below. To help you, the first words have capital letters.

1. squeaks bike needs it because My oiling .

2. women elevator tried Thirty into to the squeeze .

3. time had Everybody a at party great the .

4. are in Ducks flooded quacking creek the .

5. banquet held was The wedding church in our hall .

My score ⬚/10 Brilliant!

Lesson 48

For the tutor

The sound "ch" was introduced earlier in this program. Sometimes you need the letter "t" as well to make the same sound. Today's sight words are "watch" and "once".

witch

hatch

watch

Choose the correct words in brackets.

1. Once the (hatch match) was over, we returned home.

2. Mum is buying me a (watch catch) for my birthday.

3. A (ditch witch) was flying over the roof on a broom.

4. (Patch Latch) up the quilt with matching cotton.

5. Hungry workers ate a (batch botch) of cream cakes.

match

Read the list of words and write in the one that fits best.

1. We _____ owned a different kind of car.

2. Dig the _____ quickly before the rain starts.

3. This rabbit _____ needs frequent cleaning.

4. _____ the gate or the chickens will get out.

5. Rub your _____ sores with this ointment.

List

hutch

itchy

latch

once

ditch

My score ⬚/10 Great reading!

Choose the correct words in brackets.

1. That (stitch sketch) of a haunted house is great!

2. Try not to (snatch scratch) yourself on the face.

3. The (clutch clinch) on our car no longer works.

4. Turn off the (witch switch) before leaving the room.

5. The quins wore (matching patching) shirts and pants.

Now add the missing letters if you can. It is a good idea to read the whole sentence to find meaning clues.

1. Three c _ tches were dropped in the first inning.

2. Elastic will str _ tch if you tug it from both ends.

3. Dad w _ tched the baby while Mum did the laundry.

4. I'll need cru _ ches when I come out of hospital.

5. Curt sn _ tched food from his little brother and sister.

My score ⬚/10 Impressive!

Fish Game 9

• Photocopy and cut into squares. The aim is to find rhyming pairs.
• Deal out 6 cards each. Put the remaining cards in a pile between players.
• Have the first go to model the procedure.
• Example: "I have mice, do you have the word that rhymes?" A correct match earns another turn and returns the matching pair to the pile. An incorrect match loses a turn.
• The player to lose all their cards first, wins.

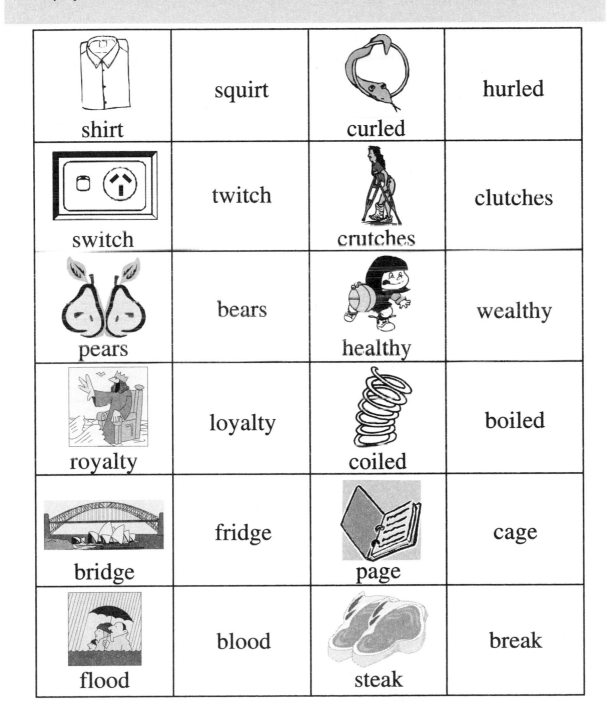

	squirt		hurled
shirt		curled	
switch	twitch	crutches	clutches
pears	bears	healthy	wealthy
royalty	loyalty	coiled	boiled
bridge	fridge	page	cage
flood	blood	steak	break

Lesson 49

For the tutor

When two vowels are joined together, the first letter is usually heard as a long vowel, for example "pain" and "leaf". In some words the first vowel has a short sound. Look at the pictures for examples.

deadly

wealth

Choose the correct words in brackets. Our sight words are "glass", "grass", and "class".

1. The teacher (read lead) a great story to our class yesterday.

2. We found the carcass of a (deaf dead) rat in the engine.

3. I wouldn't like to be attacked by a wild (bear tear).

4. The (head deaf) woman turned off her hearing aid.

5. Watch out for traffic on the road (behead ahead).

Well done! Now read the words and write the one that fits best in the space available.

	List
	heavy
	lead
	bread
	wear
	sweat

1. _____ is wasted if you burn your toast.

2. Digging ditches is very _____ work.

3. These jeans should stretch as you _____ them.

4. I _____ when I run in a long distance race.

5. _____ is a poison, so do not swallow it.

My score ☐/10 Impressive!

There are lots of interesting words using the sound "ea". Here are some of them. Choose the correct words in brackets.

1. (Heather Weather) grows wild in parts of Scotland.

2. Who's (threading treading) dirt all over the carpet?

3. (Wealthy Healthy) people drink a glass of milk daily.

4. Help Mum (dread spread) butter on the sliced bread.

5. Take a deep (breath sweater) before diving underwater.

Way to go! Lastly, add the missing letters. Don't forget to read the whole sentence for meaning clues.

1. Our school came third in the br _ ast stroke relay.

2. Heather was bitten by a d _ adly snake in the grass.

3. Dad was grumpy because his steak was dre _ adful.

4. Mitch will be punished for _ wearing at the teacher.

5. Would you prefer bacon and eggs for b _ eakfast?

My score ☐/10 You are definitely improving!

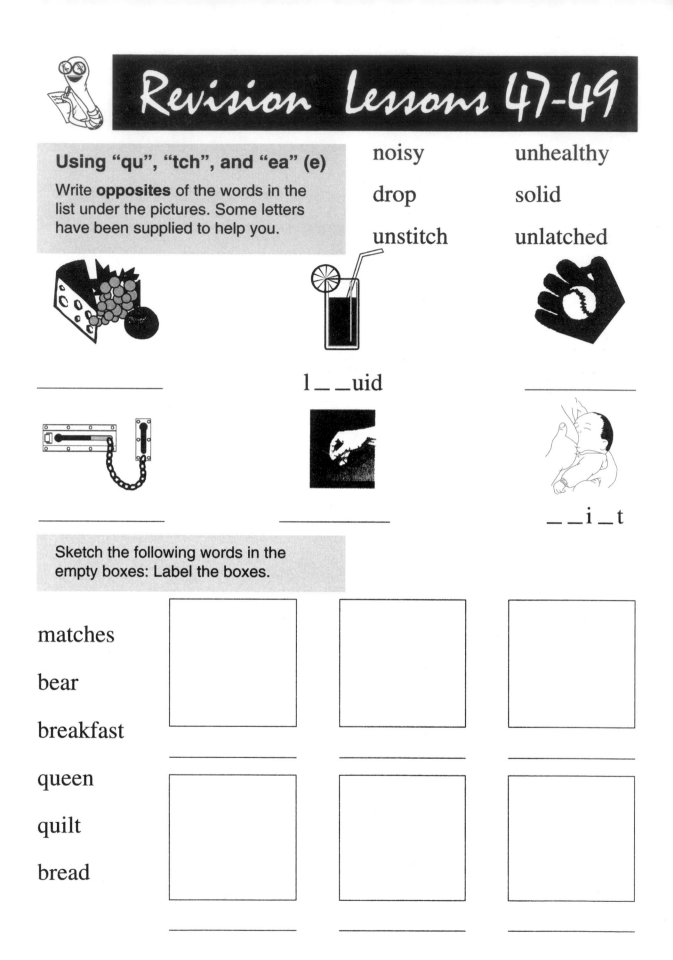

Using "qu", "tch", and "ea" (e)

Write **opposites** of the words in the list under the pictures. Some letters have been supplied to help you.

noisy   unhealthy

drop   solid

unstitch   unlatched

_____   l _ _uid   _____

_____   _____   _ _i _ t

Sketch the following words in the empty boxes: Label the boxes.

matches

bear

breakfast

queen

quilt

bread

Lesson 50

Using "ue", "ew", "y"
(short "i")
sight words: sure cruel

For the tutor
The letter combinations "ue" and "ew" can make a long "u" sound or an "oo" sound. The letter "y" sometimes makes a short "i" sound. Look at the pictures for examples. Today's sight words are "sure" and "cruel".

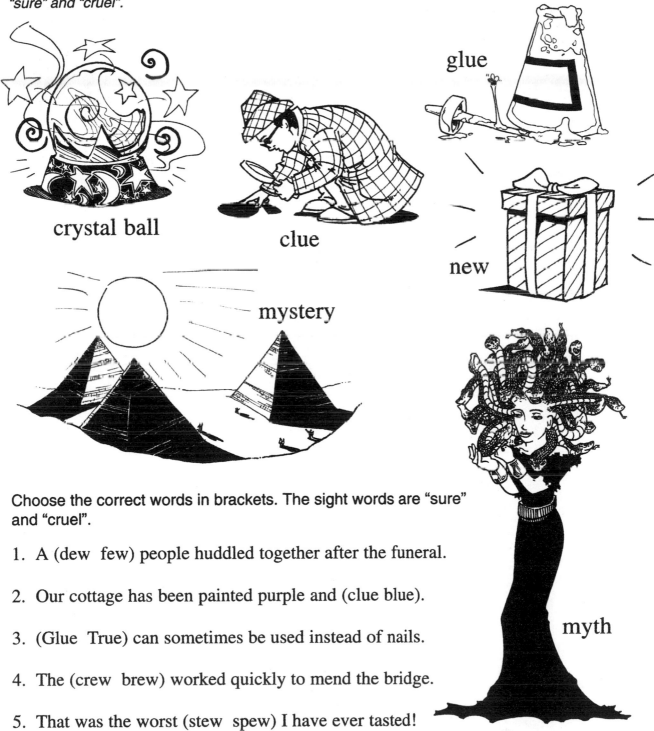

crystal ball

clue

glue

new

mystery

myth

Choose the correct words in brackets. The sight words are "sure" and "cruel".

1. A (dew few) people huddled together after the funeral.

2. Our cottage has been painted purple and (clue blue).

3. (Glue True) can sometimes be used instead of nails.

4. The (crew brew) worked quickly to mend the bridge.

5. That was the worst (stew spew) I have ever tasted!

Good reading! Read the list of words and decide where to write them.

List

1. Did you hear the _____ about the death threats?

    sure

2. Vandals were _____ for damage to property.

    flew

3. The wealthy man _____ his own helicopter.

    sued

4. Are you quite _____ they are not toadstools?

    chew

5. _____ your steak well or you may choke on it.

    news

My score ☐/10 Well done!

Let's try some more challenging words now. Don't forget that the letter "y" can make a short "i" sound. Choose the correct words in brackets.

1. Sue (threw chew) some stale bread to the blackbirds.

2. The crew was (rescued unglued) from the burning ship.

3. We were most impressed with the new football (value venue).

4. Village streets were (stewed strewn) with garbage.

5. Police solved the (myth mystery) of the forged notes.

Super! Now add the missing letters. You may need to read the whole sentence to find meaning clues.

1. The fortune teller looked deep into her cr _ stal ball.

2. Use a sk _ wer to check that the turkey is cooked.

3. Stewart is really cru _ el to animals.

4. The queen wore her jew _ ls to the royal banquet.

5. Please cont _ nue to eat your breakfast while I wait.

My score ☐/10 You did it!

Lesson 51

**Using "ph" (f) and "o"
(short "u")
sight word: among**

For the tutor

The letters "ph" make the sound "f". The letter "o" can make the same sound as a short "u", as we have already seen in Lesson 39. Look at the picture words below. Today's sight word is "among".

dove

love

trophy

photo

elephant

alphabet

Choose the correct word in brackets and circle it.

1. A white (dove love) flew over the cottage.

2. Glue the (phone photo) in the front of the album.

3. Mum baked a cake in the (oven govern).

4. (Shove Glove) the broken crystal beads into the bin.

5. The (lover plover) laid its clutch of eggs under a hedge.

phone

Good work! Read the list of words and write in the correct answers. You may need to read the whole sentence for meaning clues.

1. _____ your body with plenty of sunscreen.

2. An _____ has no mother or father.

3. _____ is the fastest athlete in the world.

4. The plane flew well _____ the clouds.

5. We could share the jewels _____ ourselves.

List

Ralph

cover

orphan

above

among

My score [/10] Keep it up!

Here are some more difficult words for you to tackle. Choose the correct word in brackets and circle it.

1. Two boys (shovelled shoved) each other off the stage.

2. Our (elephant alphabet) has twenty six letters.

3. The new boxing champ won a crystal (trophy photo).

4. Phil collects (Phantom pheasant) comics for a hobby.

5. What did you (recover discover) about Greek myths?

Terrific! Now add the missing letters. Remember, it is a good idea to read the whole sentence to find meaning clues.

1. The el _ phant was exhausted after hauling timber.

2. Stewart was orp _ aned at the age of thirteen.

3. Has your father rec _ vered from surgery to his back?

4. My ph _ tograph of a swooping hawk shared first prize.

5. Sue loves to sm _ ther her meat pie with tomato sauce.

My score [/10] You are amazing!

Using "o" (short "u") and "ph"("f")

Draw pictures of the following words in the empty boxes. Label the boxes.

glove

trophy

photo

shovel

elephant

The answers to the questions are in this list of words.

money	plover
shove	Columbus
alphabet	orphan

1. Who discovered America? _

2. What name is given to a child with no mother or father? _ _ _ _ _ _ _ _

3. What is another word for push? _ _ _ _ _ _ _ _ _ _ _ _ _ _ _ _ _

4. Which bird makes its nest on the ground? _ _ _ _ _ _ _ _ _ _ _ _

5. What has 26 letters? _

6. What does a wealthy person have plenty of? _ _ _ _ _ _ _ _ _ _ _

Lesson 52

For the tutor

The letters "air" make the sound "air". There are some examples on this page. Our sight words are "accident", "pretty", and "garage".

pair

hair

repair

Choose the correct word in brackets and circle it. (You may need to model how to sound out words, for example, ar-tis-tic).

1. Everyone loves this fresh mountain (air lair).

2. Joy has curly blonde (fair hair) and sparkling blue eyes.

3. I left a (pair air) of leather gloves in the telephone booth.

4. Balloons flew above the (lair fair) ground on Tuesday.

5. Little children usually adore reading (fairy dairy) tales.

chair

Well done! Read the list of words and write in the correct answers.

List

1. We may cover the _____ case with new carpet.

   pretty

2. _____ of elephants hauled timber to the river.

   hairy

3. I am _____ sure my photo will win first prize.

   lairs

4. Hunters trapped a number of foxes in their _____ .

   pairs

5. Spider monkeys have small, _____ bodies.

   stair

My score ◻/10 Great!

Now for some more words using the sound "air". Choose the correct word in brackets and circle it. (*You may need to explain the word "flair"*).

1. Artistic (flair chair) is needed to carve marble statues.

2. The garage was unable to (unfair repair) our clutch.

3. Some animals are completely (airless hairless).

4. Princess Grace was the (fairest fairer) of them all.

5. We are (fairly fairy) confident we will win a few trophies.

Correct! Now fill in the missing letters. Don't forget to read the whole sentence to find meaning clues.

1. Where did your mother buy this lovely leather c _ air?

2. Two dreadful acc _ dents were caused by bad weather.

3. Claire was unf _ irly blamed for breaking the crystal glass.

4. There are long delays at the air _ ort because of heavy fog.

5. Ralph is re _ airing the damage done by vandals.

My score ◻/10 That was excellent reading!

Lesson 53

Using "ie" (long "e")
"u" (oo)
sight word: through

For the tutor

In an earlier lesson, I explained that when two vowels are joined together, the first one usually makes a long vowel sound. Today we will be learning some words where this rule is not followed. Look at the pictures to see what I mean.

push

grief

chief

thief

Our sight word today is "through".
Choose the correct word in brackets and circle it.

1. What was the (chief grief) reason for the accident?

2. Local farmers plant their (fields yields) with wheat.

3. A (brief thief) stole the wealthy woman's jewels.

4. It was a (belief relief) when the repairs were done.

5. There was only a (grief brief) delay at the airport.

retriever

Well done! Choose the word that fits best and write it in the space provided.

List

1. Alice stepped _____ the looking glass.

2. The mother elephant _____ for her dead baby.

3. A phantom appeared _____ in my dream.

4. Philip would not _____ a word I said.

5. Police are sure they will catch the _____ .

List

briefly

through

grieved

thieves

believe

My score ⬜/10 That was pretty easy for you!

Choose the correct word in brackets and circle it.

1. Our (retriever reliever) loves to fetch balls and sticks.

2. Susie (pushed bushed) the packages off the armchair.

3. The (priest briefcase) made his sermon quite interesting.

4. Where did you leave your woollen (pullover bulldozer)?

5. The officer (fielded shielded) himself from the gunfire.

Terrific! Now add the missing letters. Read the whole sentence to find meaning clues.

1. Hurry thr _ ugh the turnstile before the shop is full of people.

2. Connie didn't bel _ eve my story about a hairy monster.

3. Two unlucky gold miners were amb _ shed by thieves.

4. I shri _ ked with terror when the staircase collapsed.

5. Everyone was rel _ eved when the money was recovered.

Did you notice that some words ending with "f" changed when made plural or into a verb? For example, "thief" became "thieves" and "belief" became "believe".

My score ⬜/10 You are a legend!

Fish Game 10

• The rules for this Fish Game are the same as the rhyming fish games. See Fish Game 9 on page 171.

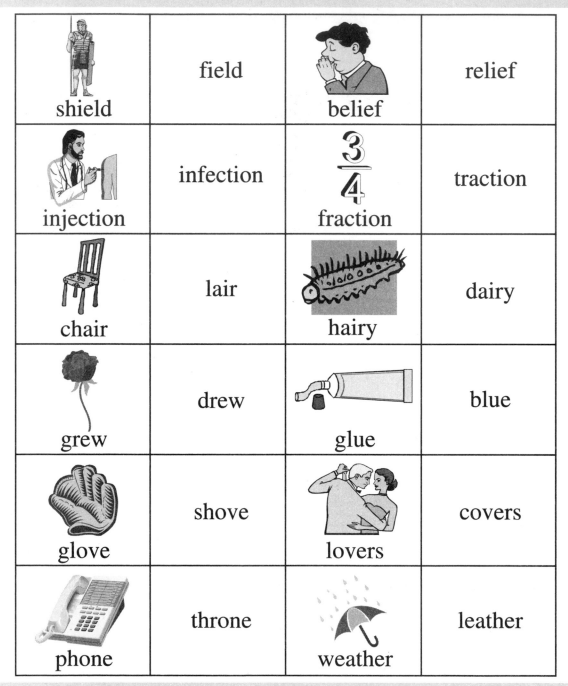

shield	field	belief	relief
injection	infection	fraction	traction
chair	lair	hairy	dairy
grew	drew	glue	blue
glove	shove	lovers	covers
phone	throne	weather	leather

• Try making your own cards with the following words: crying, drying, fried, tried, launch, paunch, draw, straw, barrow, sparrow, pillow, willow, felon, melon, season, reason, school, pool, book, took, crawling, drawling, haunted, taunted. If you want, you can illustrate your cards.

Lesson 54

For the tutor

Today's lesson is really challenging. We will be learning about words using "sion" and "tion" to make the sound "shun". Look at the pictures to see some examples. The sight word is "auction".

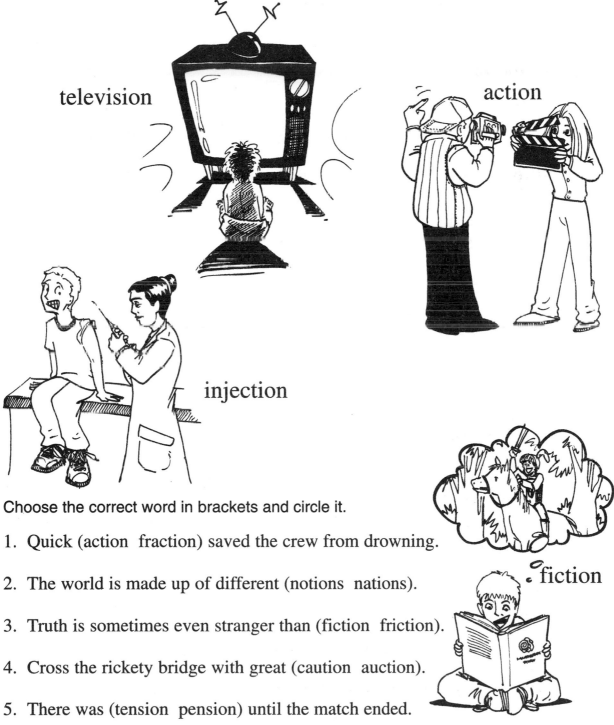

television

action

injection

fiction

Choose the correct word in brackets and circle it.

1. Quick (action fraction) saved the crew from drowning.

2. The world is made up of different (notions nations).

3. Truth is sometimes even stranger than (fiction friction).

4. Cross the rickety bridge with great (caution auction).

5. There was (tension pension) until the match ended.

You did it! Now choose the word that fits best and write it in the space provided.

1. Blair had an accident at the railway _____ .

2. My wealthy uncle lives in a huge _____ .

3. This _____ should help relieve itching.

4. Mum wants to buy a chair at the _____ .

5. Did I _____ that I saw three deer today?

My score ⬜/10 Fantastic reading!

Here are some more words using "tion" and "sion" to make the sound "shun". If you get stuck, sound out, look for smaller words inside the longer words, or read on. Choose the correct word in brackets and circle it.

1. The vet gave my sick puppy an (infection injection).

2. Kelly's leg was in (fraction traction) after the accident.

3. Check the meaning of words in a (television dictionary).

4. This store has a good (selection confection) of videos.

5. Dad's stamp (collection reduction) is worth a fortune.

Finally, see if you can unscramble the sentences. Do it orally first, then write down your answers below.

1. watch Did television you Saturday on ?

2. broken burglars The into mansion was by .

3. insects by can Infections spread be .

4. the to Oil engine friction prevent .

5. any Are doing fractions good you at ?

My score ⬜/10 Excellent!

The Yeti

High in the mountains of Tibet, Terry Cooper was on the trail of a yeti. His plan was to capture one in a cage and charge everyone to see it. He was sure he would make a fortune!

People in the villages stared in amazement as Terry hurried past. His poor team followed, weighed down with heavy packs, and at the rear was the bamboo cage hauled by a yak. Terry was heading for a distant valley where he believed a yeti might live.

When they reached the valley, Terry set up camp. However, there was only one small tent, so his exhausted team had to sleep out in the open air. Just before dark, the cage was concealed in a thick clump of bushes. A live hare was trapped inside to tempt the yeti out of hiding.

Early next morning, Terry approached the cage. He was surprised to see a note tied to the door frame. It said: "Many thanks for the yummy breakfast!"

> *concealed: Try reading to the end of the sentence…This word means the same as "hidden". The second "c" sounds like "s".*
>
> *early: This word is the opposite of "late".*

Here is a quiz for you to try.
Answer yes or no to each question.

1. An action is something that is done. _____

2. A thief is a person who can be trusted with money. _____

3. Flair means to have natural talent at something. _____

4. Farmers sow crops in fields. _____

5. The opposite of fair is unfair. _____

6. A shield is used to repair a chair. _____

7. An injection is given with a needle. _____

8. A fraction is a part of something. _____

9. Expansion means an increase in size. _____

10. A fairy tale is true and you can believe it. _____

• Join up the words that rhyme.

relief	blue
shielded	fairies
glue	flairs
fraction	cover
dairies	pension
brew	nation
lover	crew
stairs	belief
station	traction
tension	fielded

Lesson 55

For the tutor

Sometimes the letter "i" makes a long "e" sound. Combined with a "u", it makes an "oo" sound. Look at the pictures for examples.

kiwi

piano

alien

fruit juice

stadium

Choose the correct word in brackets and circle it.

1. A (kiwi mini) is a nocturnal bird native to New Zealand.

2. Villagers believe they saw a (pizza yeti) in the forest.

3. Healthy people eat plenty of raw (juice fruit) each day.

4. Toni felt like an (alien idiot) when she fell downstairs.

5. Stephen's photograph was taken in a (studio radio).

suit

That was great! Now read the words and write the one that fits best in the space provided. You should read the whole sentence to find meaning clues.

List

1. It is _____ to thread needles with a large hole.

2. The _____ on the beachfront sells ice-cream.

3. We sold our _____ at the auction on Tuesday.

4. Orange juice was provided during the _____ .

5. _____ was relieved to return home safely.

Fiona

kiosk

cruise

easier

piano

My score ⬜/10 That was wonderful! Keep it up!

If you get stuck, sound out, look for smaller words inside longer words, or read on. Once again, choose the correct word in brackets and circle it.

1. The Olympic (stadium radium) is nearly completed.

2. Our (stallion carrion) was given an injection yesterday.

3. Rita is just (radiant brilliant) at playing the piano.

4. The new (juicer recruit) has his leg in traction.

5. That factory is worth at least a (billion bullion) dollars.

Very impressive! Now add the missing letters. Don't forget to look for meaning clues in the sentence.

1. David is our national breast stroke champ _ on.

2. A mill _ on pamphlets were delivered to households.

3. Jasmine is very pretty, but Sharon is even pr _ ttier.

4. The aircraft carr _ er was launched on Tuesday morning.

5. An obed _ ent dog will always follow your instructions.

My score ⬜/10 You are a star!

Lesson 56

For the tutor

The letters "ous" make the sound "us". Sometimes the letter "o" makes an "oo" sound. Look at the pictures for examples. Today's sight words are "yacht" and "whose".

famous

poisonous

SLOW LANE

moves

Choose the correct word in brackets and circle it. Today's sight word is yacht.

1. Police officers ordered Mum to (move lose) her car.

2. The pianist was extremely (nervous porous).

3. (Who's Whose) dictionary is easier to use?

4. This kiosk is (famous luminous) for its great pizzas.

5. Dad was (curious furious) when our stallion was stolen.

proves

Excellent! Read the words and write in the one that fits best in the space provided.

List

1. My reading will _____ with practice.

2. It was a relief when the _____ sailed ashore.

3. We were _____ about appearing on stage.

4. Jodie is quite _____ of her prettier sister.

5. Please _____ the dead ferns from the patio.

improve

jealous

remove

yacht

nervous

My score ▱/10 Very good reading!

Some more difficult examples of the sounds we are revising appear on this page. Good luck! Choose the correct word in brackets and circle it.

1. (Fabulous Poisonous) fumes billowed from the gas works.

2. A hippo may be (jealous dangerous) if you disturb it.

3. Salt water crocodiles have (enormous nervous) jaws.

4. Sailing to Antarctica could prove (porous perilous).

5. That television program was (marvellous furious).

Great! Now add the missing letters. You should read the whole sentence to find meaning clues.

1. Have you noticed the impro _ ement in my spelling?

2. We were curi _ us to hear about Shane's crazy invention.

3. A visit to the Olympic stadium would be fab _ lous.

4. Elephants and hippos are en _ rm _ us animals.

5. Were you serio _ s about an overseas holiday next year?

My score ▱/10 Wonderful!

Unscramble the letters to fit the clues.

a n p o i   _____
A musical instrument with black and white keys

s f o a m u   _____
Very well known indeed

x m t e i u r   _____
A blend of ingredients

z l i s a e t   _____
The person who does the least work

l a c f c u r   _____
Another word for "cautious"

• Write captions under the pictures.   taught   furniture   eighteen
stallion

Lesson 57

Using "are" (air) , "oor", and "oar" (or)
sight words: obey prey grey

The letters "are" can make the sound "air". The sound "or" can be made in a number of ways including "oor" and "oar". Can you think of any others? Revise the sounds "aw" and "au" from Lesson 42. The sight words are obey, prey, and grey.

stare

hoard

scared

hare

door

Choose the correct word in brackets and circle it. The sight words are "prey", "grey", and "obey".

1. Nurses take great (dare care) of people in hospital.

2. However did you manage to drop both (roars oars)?

3. They couldn't prove they had paid their (mare fare).

4. The clothing department is through that (door boor).

5. Jessica has a fabulous collection of (bare rare) stamps.

Very good! Read the words and write in the one that fits best in the space provided.

1. Fiona _____ me to enter the championships.

2. Mum was furious when _____ ate the carrots.

3. Our flat is on the third _____ of the mansion.

4. That cocker spaniel refuses to _____ its master.

5. Eagles, falcons, and hawks are birds of _____ .

List

obey

prey

floor

hares

dared

My score ☐/10 Excellent reading!

That wasn't hard, was it? Now we can try some more difficult words using the same sounds. Choose the correct word in brackets and circle it. (*You may need to explain that a spoor is the trail or track of an animal.*)

1. The hunters are following the (floor spoor) of their prey.

2. Toddlers are sometimes (spared scared) of the dark.

3. It is rude to (stare snare) at people in wheelchairs.

4. Thieves hid the stolen loot under loose (hoards boards).

5. Grey (shared flared) trousers were once very popular.

Way to go! Finally, add the missing letters. You may need to read the whole sentence to look for meaning clues.

1. Tina is sh _ ring her sandwiches with her friends.

2. Be ca _ eful of skunks near the edge of the forest.

3. We should replace the fl _ orboards in the dining room.

4. A flar _ indicated the exact position of the sinking yacht.

5. The captain and crew are b_ arding the aircraft carrier .

My score ☐/10 Excellent reading!

Lesson 58

For the tutor

Today's lesson will help you with the sound "cher" made by the letters "ture". Look at the examples first.

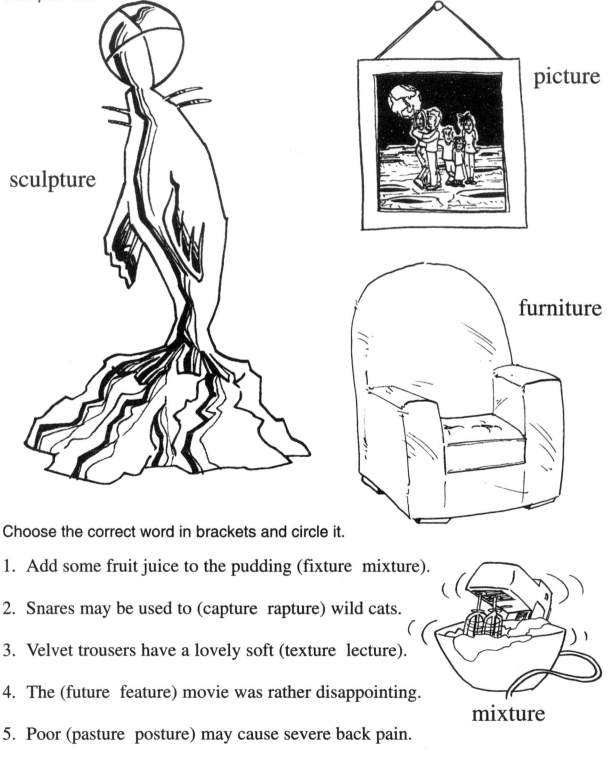

sculpture

picture

furniture

Choose the correct word in brackets and circle it.

1. Add some fruit juice to the pudding (fixture mixture).

2. Snares may be used to (capture rapture) wild cats.

3. Velvet trousers have a lovely soft (texture lecture).

4. The (future feature) movie was rather disappointing.

5. Poor (pasture posture) may cause severe back pain.

mixture

Very good! Read the words and write in the one that fits best in the space provided.

1. Shelley was _____ for spitting in public.

2. Hang the _____ above the sideboard.

3. _____ picked the carcass clean.

4. Natural fertilizer can improve our _____ .

5. In _____ , be more careful with money.

List

future

picture

vultures

pastures

lectured

My score ⬦/10 That was great!

You are doing really well with this sound, which is quite challenging. Have a go at some harder words now. Add the missing letters. You will need to read the whole sentence to find meaning clues.

1. The punct _ re was caused by riding over broken glass.

2. Children enjoy adv _ nture playground equipment.

3. Leather furn _ ture is expensive, but it lasts for ages.

4. A famous bronze sculptu   e is on display at the gallery

5. Did you hear the temperat _ re forecast for Saturday?

Terrific reading! Now try to unscramble the words to make sentences. Work out your answers orally before writing them on paper. To help you, the first words start with capital letters.

1. dropped the her Granny into sink dentures .

2. creature were of strange They the scared .

3. fractured leg fell I my over when I .

4. tasted chocolate mixture The pudding fabulous .

5. thieves Police after chase captured a the long .

My score ⬦/10 Brilliant!

Lesson 59

For the tutor

The letters "gh" can either make the sound "f", or no sound at all. In this lesson we will be revising "igh" (making a long "i") and "eigh" (making a long "a"). Our sight word is "sugar".

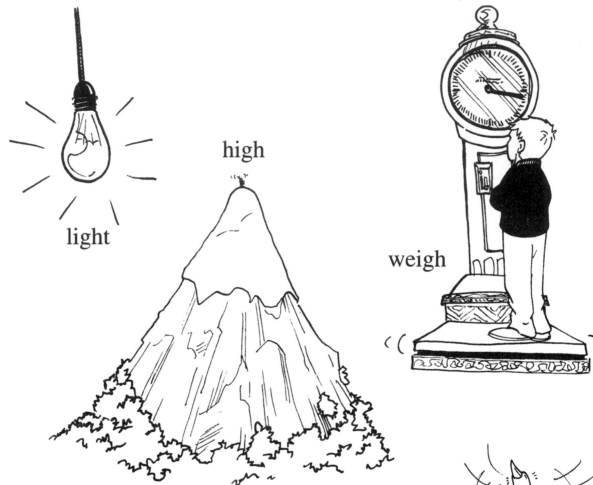

light

high

weigh

Circle the words in brackets that best fit the meaning.

1. Tracey (sighs   highs) with relief when her plane lands.

2. Quick action by doctors saved Sue's eye (might   sight).

3. (Weigh   Neigh) the mixture before adding the dried fruit.

4. Our grandmother will be (eight   eighty) next birthday.

5. Is that an eagle flying (high   nigh) above the branches?

flight

So far, so good! Now read the list of words and write in the one makes sense.

1. The _____ was hauled up the snowy slopes.

2. Philip was _____ about the dangerous fox.

3. This furniture looks _____ , but it is heavy.

4. _____ vultures swooped onto the dead lion.

5. Our helicopter _____ was an adventure.

List

light

sleigh

flight

eight

right

My score ☐/10 Terrific reading!

As you can see, the letters "gh" are tricky. Here are some more examples. If you get stuck, sound out, look for small words inside longer words, or read on to find meaning clues. Read the words and choose the one that fits best.

1. It is my brother's _____ birthday today.

2. Nocturnal creatures avoid _____ sunshine.

3. Our holiday in Western _____ was great.

4. _____ trains carry goods across the Mid-West.

5. I was _____ when we won the trophy.

List

Canada

bright

freight

eighteenth

delighted

Very good! Now add the missing letters. You should read the whole sentence to find meaning clues.

1. It would be del _ ghtful to travel around Texas.

2. Ralph missed his fli _ ht to London because of heavy fog.

3. The hoard of gold we _ ghed at least three tonnes.

4. My mare neig _ ed as I approached with sugar cubes.

5. That picture hanging over the fireplace is frigh _ ful.

My score ☐/10 Wonderful!

Lesson 60

For the tutor

In the last lesson, we looked at words with a silent "gh". This time the lesson is about other ways of using the same letters.

laugh

bough

RRR

tough

Today's sight word is "laugh". As you can see, "gh" can make the sound "f". Read the sentences and circle the words that make sense.

daughter

1. Ruth (fought bought) a stuffed bobcat at the auction.

2. Complain to the butcher if the steak is too (rough tough).

3. When were you (naught taught) to ride the stallion?

4. Jackals (sought fought) over the carcass of the zebra.

5. Police (caught taught) eight thieves on Thursday night.

Read the words and write them in the spaces provided. You will need to read the sentences first to find meaning clues.

1. Jake's adventures in Colorado made everyone _____ .

2. These floorboards have quite a _____ surface.

3. I _____ fresh cheese sandwiches from home.

4. The west produces more than _____ wheat.

5. Mum _____ new kitchen furniture today.

List:
laugh
brought
rough
enough
bought

My score ☐/10 That was easy for you!

There are other ways to use "gh". For example, "ough" makes the sound "ow" in "bough", but long "o" in "though". Confusing, isn't it? My advice if you are stuck is to look for meaning clues in the sentence. Read the words and choose the one that fits best.

1. The _____ of baby seals is monstrous.

2. Everybody _____ at the Halloween pumpkin.

3. We attached the swing to a _____ on the tree.

4. Their baby _____ is weighed monthly.

5. I _____ there were raccoons in the rafters.

List:
bough
daughter
slaughter
thought
laughed

Lastly, add the missing letters if you can.

1. It was thou _ htful of you to fix the puncture in my bike wheel.

2. Children were l _ ughing at the clown's comic actions.

3. Althou _ h the steak is tough, it is still quite tasty.

4. Are you sure there are en _ ugh oysters for the banquet?

5. The sl _ ughter house floor was slippery and dangerous.

My score ☐/10 Excellent reading!

Lesson 61

For the tutor

You already know that vowels can make different sounds depending on the letters they are used with. In this lesson, we are revising the vowel "a" used as a short "o". The sight words are all contractions, that is, two words shortened into one. Can you work out what the two words are in the examples?

swan

waddle

wasp

wallaby

Read the words and write them in the correct space.

	List
	wand
	swap
	don't
	wasp
	swans

1. Shield yourself or the _____ might sting.

2. _____ forget to weigh the flour and sugar first.

3. Black _____ may attack in the breeding season.

4. He waved his _____ and a rabbit appeared.

5. Can I _____ these pictures for something else?

Now add the missing letters if you can.

1. The champion w _ n't be able to compete in his event.

2. Sw _ t the flies before they lay their eggs.

3. I c _ n't remember who taught me how to ride a bike.

4. Toddlers are likely to wa _ der off if left unattended.

5. The light bulb has a strength of 60 w _ tts.

My score ◻/10 Very good reading!

You are doing really well. Now let's try some more difficult words using the letter "a" to make a short "o" sound. Read the list words and write them in the correct space.

List

1. My sore throat makes it difficult to _____ .

wallabies

2. My mum serves _____ with roast beef.

squash

3. Eight _____ are grazing in the bushes.

waddle

4. Ducks _____ on land but are graceful in water.

swallow

5. I left my leather _____ at the stadium.

wallet

Unscramble the words to make sentences. Do this orally before writing the answers below. The first words have capital letters.

1. swapped was Grandpa because deaf seats he .

2. house the enjoyed Everyone butterfly wandering the around .

3. you swallow barn the Did see in the ?

4. caterpillar by was unlucky swallowed a The sparrow .

5. waddled Two staircase ladies up fat the .

My score ◻/10 Excellent!

Lesson 62

For the tutor
There are many words with silent letters. This lesson will help you recognize them.

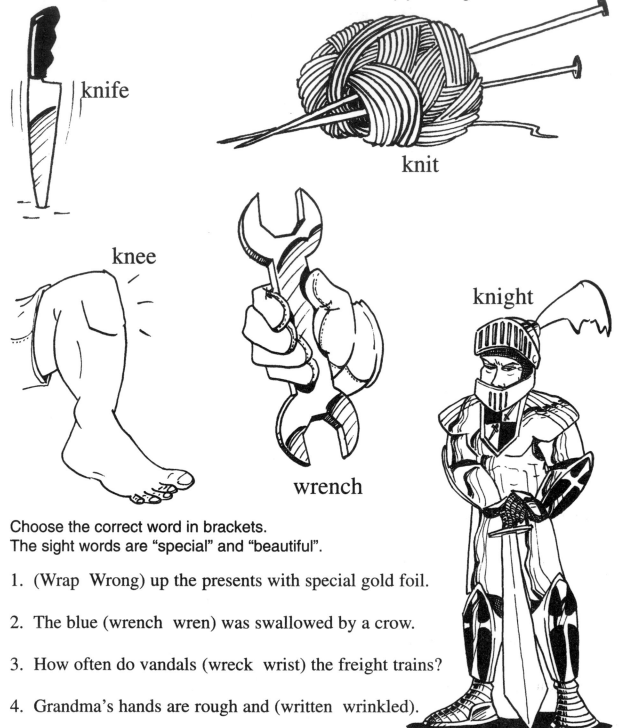

knife

knit

knee

wrench

knight

Choose the correct word in brackets.
The sight words are "special" and "beautiful".

1. (Wrap Wrong) up the presents with special gold foil.

2. The blue (wrench wren) was swallowed by a crow.

3. How often do vandals (wreck wrist) the freight trains?

4. Grandma's hands are rough and (written wrinkled).

5. Stephen placed a (wreath wretch) on the gravestone.

Good work! Read the words and then fill in the gaps.

List

1. Worms _____ through the damp soil.
   wriggle

2. Mum has promised a _____ birthday treat.
   wrote

3. I _____ my ankle during the match.
   special

4. Dad _____ a feature story for the newspaper.
   wrenched

5. It is _____ to capture native animals for sale.
   wrong

My score ⬜/10 Very good reading!

The letter "k" is sometimes silent. Here are some examples. Choose the correct word in brackets.

1. Sharpen your (knee knife) before carving tough meat.

2. The brave (night knight) had many amazing adventures.

3. Ask the teacher if you don't (no know) how to do it.

4. Tighten up the (knots knits) or they may come undone.

5. It is polite to (knock knack) before entering a house.

Try to fill in the missing letters. Remember, it is a good idea to read the whole sentence to look for meaning clues.

1. Our world is full of strange and bea _ tiful creatures.

2. Sandra took months to kn _ t a scarf and sweater.

3. I grazed both k _ ees when I jumped off the bulldozer.

4. The burglars left clear fingerprints on the door _ nob.

5. My knapsa _ k was heavy because it was full of supplies.

My score ⬜/10 That was great!

Lesson 63

For the tutor

The letters "h", "b", "g", and "c" are sometimes silent. Look at the pictures to see what I mean.

ghost

gnaw

bomb

gnat

scent

climb

Choose the correct word in brackets. The first two sets use a silent "h" and "b". Today's sight words are "warm" and "wardrobe".

1. This beautiful jumper took eighteen (ours hours) to knit.

2. Roast (limb lamb) tastes wonderful with mint sauce.

3. A dangerous (tomb bomb) exploded in the station.

4. Sarah gave stale bread (crumbs thumbs) to the geese.

5. Do not attempt the steep (comb climb) without ropes.

hour

Read the words and fill in the gaps.

1. Can you read the writing on the _____ ?

2. A _____ can move with lightning speed.

3. Fetch me a _____ blanket from the wardrobe.

4. Paul thought he saw a _____ in the attic.

5. An _____ person always tells the truth.

cheetah

honest

warm

ghost

tombstone

My score ⬜/10 Super!

The letters "g" and "c" are also silent sometimes. Choose the correct word in brackets.
(*You may need to explain what "gnat" is.*)

1. Our garden (gnome gnat) was knocked over by dogs.

2. The (sign science) post pointed in the wrong direction.

3. The parfume I bought had a lovely (ascent scent).

4. You need sharp (scissors scenery) to cut heavy material.

5. The pup (gnaws knits) on his meaty bone for hours.

Fill in the missing letters. Don't forget to read the whole sentence to find meaning clues.
(*You may need to explain what "gnash" means.*)

1. A g _ at is an annoying, blood-sucking insect.

2. Laura's s _ ience experiment resulted in an explosion.

3. Nana clutches the banisters as she des _ ends the stairs.

4. Can we desi _ n our own magazine cover for a project?

5. Phil _ nashes his teeth when he gets really frustrated.

My score ⬜/10 That was excellent reading!

Lesson 64

For the tutor

This is the last lesson on silent letters; we will be looking at the letters "u" and "t".

wrestle

castle

guitar

guinea pig

Choose the correct word in brackets.

1. Scotch (whistles thistles) are covered with prickles.

2. Did you know this (castle bustle) is haunted by ghosts?

3. The (wrestle trestle) is covered with objects for sale.

4. My uncle has just bought an electric (guitar guinea pig).

5. (Guest Guess) the weight of the turkey and win a prize.

Good work! Read the words and write in the correct answer.

List

1. My attempt at making _____ was a flop.   guilty

                                                              guard

2. Nobody would _____ to her weak excuses.   listen

                                                              build

3. The judge sentenced the _____ man to death.   biscuits

4. Crocodiles _____ their hatchlings closely.

5. We must _____ a cage for the guinea pigs.

My score ☐/10 Great work! You are doing really well.

• Join up the words that rhyme.

guilt	host
dumb	won't
don't	squashed
written	twaddle
gnawing	sight
knight	numb
wrapping	pawing
washed	built
waddle	kitten
ghost	mapping

• Write captions under the pictures.

knife   knapsack
kneeling   castle

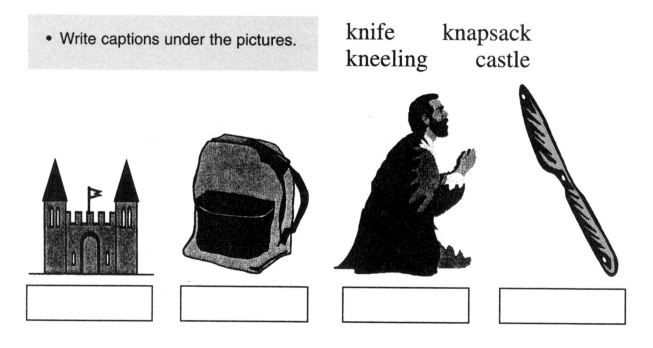

Lesson 65

Using "alk" (ork),
"ear" (er), and "our" (or)
sight words: wolf shoes

For the tutor

In this lesson, we will be revising the sounds made by the letters "alk", "ear", and "our". The sight words are "wolf" and "shoes".

pearl

earth

tournament

chalk

Many of these words will already be familiar to you. The tricky part is how to spell them! Choose the correct word in brackets.

1. A naughty child threw (talk chalk) at the blackboard.

2. (Walk Balk) carefully to avoid thistles and stinging nettles.

3. Remove those tough (stalks chalks) with a sharp knife.

4. They built (pour four) go-karts, but one was wrecked.

5. Astronauts flew their spacecraft above the (earl Earth).

pour

Way to go! Read the words and complete the sentences.

List

1. Why are you frightened the _____ will attack?

2. My new leather shoes squeaked as I _____ .

3. It took months to _____ how to knit properly.

4. We watched the cheetah as it _____ its prey.

5. The volleyball _____ is covered in puddles.

stalked

wolf

learn

court

walked

My score ⊿/10 Well done!

That was pretty easy for you. Now try some more words using the same sounds. Read the words and then fill in the spaces provided.

List

1. These fabulous _____ are worth a fortune!

2. The wizard _____ footsteps outside his castle.

3. The children _____ the death of their pony.

4. I won a lovely trophy in the _____.

5. I'm going skating on my _____ birthday.

fourteenth

pearls

mourned

tournament

heard

Great! Now fill in the missing letters. You may need to read the whole sentence to find meaning clues.

1. Using a dictionary helps us le _ rn the meaning of words.

2. Because of the po _ ring rain, my shoes were soaked.

3. The umpire should have blown his whistle much ear _ ier.

4. Casey came equal f _ urth in the photography competition.

5. The wolf was sta _ king a herd of deer grazing nearby.

My score ⊿/10 Excellent reading!

Lesson 66

For the tutor

The letters "ou" normally make the sound "ow" as in "cow". However, they can also make the sound "or" when combined with the letter "r". We looked at some examples in the last lesson. Today's lesson shows two other sounds made by "ou".

young

group

tourist

Choose the correct words in brackets. The sight word is "color".

1. Eighteen (tourists toucans) explored the castle grounds.

2. A (group route) of beginners entered the tournament.

3. The search party found the missing (coupon youth).

4. Several men were (wounded wounding) by stray bullets.

5. A (tour troupe) of monkeys stripped the branches bare.

couple

Well done! Now fill in the missing letters. You may need to read the whole sentence to find meaning clues.

1. Wrap the w _ und tightly to avoid further loss of blood.

2. The quickest ro _ te would be through the valley.

3. The bus to _ r visited the ancient Roman ruins.

4. Cut around the edges of this co _ pon with scissors.

5. Although she is nearly eighty, Nana still feels you _ hful.

My score ⬜/10 That was great!

As you can see, "ou" can make the sound "oo". Now we will look at "ou" making a short "u" sound, as in "cup". Read the words and write them in the correct spaces.

List

flourish

trouble

couples

country

cousin

1. Married _____ usually go on honeymoon.

2. Those youths are in _____ with the police.

3. Tourists love visiting our beautiful _____ .

4. My _____ gobbled up most of the fruit.

5. Climbing vines _____ in a sunny position.

Very good! Now fill in the missing letters. You may need to read the whole sentence to find meaning clues.

1. John spends hours c _ loring in pictures in magazines.

2. It is unwise to to _ ch the prickly stalks of Scotch thistles.

3. Ruth and Tony won the mixed dou _ les championship.

4. It took great c _ urage to climb the snowy mountain peak.

5. All mammals no _ rish their young babies with milk.

My score ⬜/10 You did it!

Lesson 67

Using "oul" (ol)
"ch" (sh and k)
sight word: sew

For the tutor

When you combine "ou" with an "l", you make the sound "ol" ("could", "would", and "should" are exceptions). The letters "ch" sometimes sound like "sh" or "k". Look at these examples.

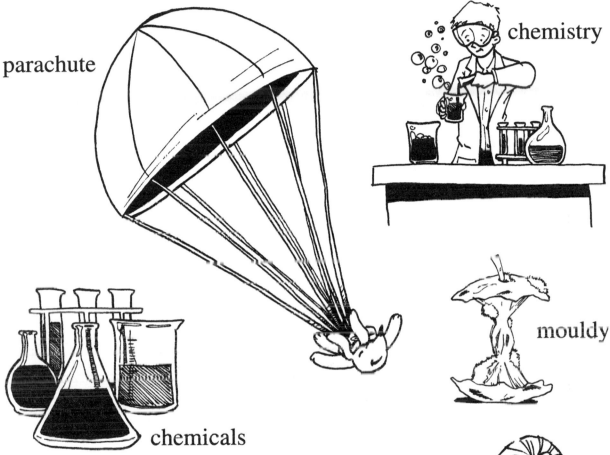

parachute

chemistry

chemicals

mouldy

Choose the correct word in brackets.

1. The motel (chimp chef) is honest and hard-working.

2. I wrenched my (boulder shoulder) playing basketball.

3. The starving dog gnawed a (mouldy moulting) bone.

4. My wrists (ached echoed) after wrapping the presents.

5. You must not touch those dangerous (chords chemicals).

shoulders

Correct! Now read the words and write them in the spaces.

1. Mum had to _____ thousands of sequins on my vest.

2. A huge _____ blocked the mountain pass.

3. Our voices _____ in the underground cavern.

4. Will the guests arrive on _____ eve?

5. _____ sometimes grows on food in the fridge.

List

Christmas

sew

echoed

mould

boulder

My score ⬚ /10 You did it!

There are some more examples of words using "oul" and "ch" below. Fill in the missing letters. You may need to read the whole sentence to find meaning clues.

1. A c _ ameleon is a lizard that can change color quickly.

2. The pilot floated safely to earth on his para _ _ ute.

3. Embers from your camp fire may sm _ ulder for hours.

4. Christine has decided to study Ch _ mistry in college.

5. The biscuits are even mo _ ldier than the stale bread.

Well done! Now try to unscramble the words to make sentences. Work out the answers orally before writing them down. To help you, the first word in each sentence has a capital letter.

1. ached finished My when legs the I marathon .

2. landslide were boulders the in dislodged Many .

3. menu The offering chef a tonight is special .

4. some at Buy ointment pharmacy the .

5. in apple found Mum my mouldy wardrobe a .

My score ⬚ /10 You are a star!

Lesson 68

For the tutor

This is the last lesson in the program. We will be looking at the letter "g" making the sound "j" and the letter "c" making the sound "s". The sight words are "cough" and "recipe".

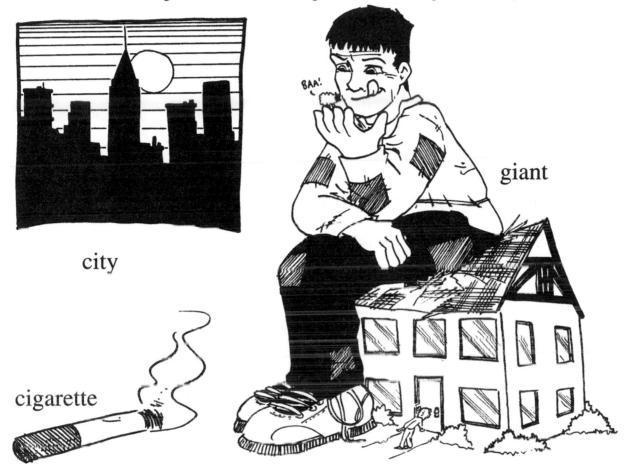

city

giant

cigarette

Choose the correct words in brackets.

1. Our family lives in the centre of the (cemetery city).

2. Guards formed a (century circle) to protect the castle.

3. This chocolate pudding recipe looks (excellent exciting).

4. The angry (genius giant) stomped on the terrified crowd.

5. Be (gentle generous) when you touch baby animals.

circle

Fine work! Now read the words and fill in the spaces.

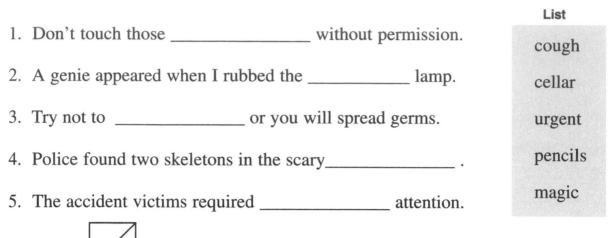

List

1. Don't touch those _____ without permission.

2. A genie appeared when I rubbed the _____ lamp.

3. Try not to _____ or you will spread germs.

4. Police found two skeletons in the scary_____ .

5. The accident victims required _____ attention.

cough

cellar

urgent

pencils

magic

My score ⟋10 Way to go!

Here are some more words using "g" and "c". If you get stuck, sound out, look for smaller words inside the longer words, or read on to find meaning clues. Choose the correct words in brackets.

1. Smoking (celery cigarettes) is really bad for your health.

2. A (giraffe general) escaped from its zoo enclosure today.

3. An (emergency urgency) siren interrupted the concert.

4. (Cyclones Centipedes) have caused many shipwrecks.

5. Our electric (generator general) needs urgent repairs.

Wonderful! Lastly, add the missing letters.

1. My birthday present was wrapped in orange celloph _ ne.

2. It is nec _ ssary to carry flares when sailing a yacht.

3. Are you c _ rtain that these chemicals are not dangerous?

4. A gigant _ c explosion rocked buildings throughout the city.

5. Christmas is celebrat _ d in many countries in the world.

My score ⟋10 Congratulations!

Castle in the Sky

Peering through the windows, I could see the cables that connected the castle to huge boulders far below. For some strange reason, the countryside reminded me of a picture in a fairy tale.

I joined a group of tourists admiring the fabulous treasures on display. Many pieces of furniture were made of gold, and the enormous dining table was set with crystal glasses and silver candlesticks. A collection of pearl and jade necklaces on the sideboard must have been worth a fortune.

After a while, to my delight, I discovered a secret courtyard. Birds sang and the sweet scent of flowers filled the air. I sat down on the grass and soon drifted off to sleep.

Suddenly, an unpleasant noise made my head ache. It grew louder and more urgent. What on earth could it be?

"Hurry up or you will be late for school. Your alarm went off ages ago!" yelled Mum.

Congratulations! You have successfully completed the phonics program!

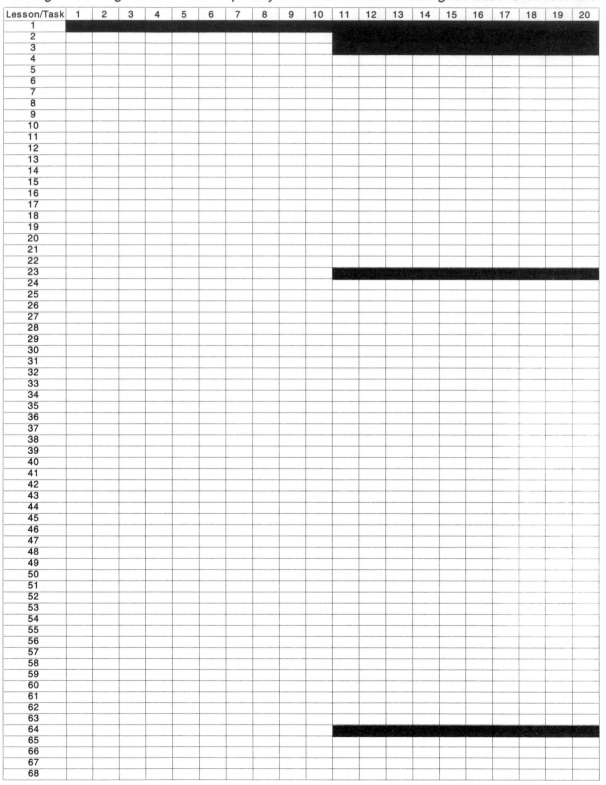

Lesson Score Card

Using one color for correct and a different color for incorrect, color in the squares according to how you do in each individual task for every lesson. This chart can be photocopied to a larger size and be hung on the fridge or other visible spot in your home. You can reward good lessons with stickers.

Lesson/Task	1	2	3	4	5	6	7	8	9	10	11	12	13	14	15	16	17	18	19	20
1																				
2																				
3																				
4																				
5																				
6																				
7																				
8																				
9																				
10																				
11																				
12																				
13																				
14																				
15																				
16																				
17																				
18																				
19																				
20																				
21																				
22																				
23																				
24																				
25																				
26																				
27																				
28																				
29																				
30																				
31																				
32																				
33																				
34																				
35																				
36																				
37																				
38																				
39																				
40																				
41																				
42																				
43																				
44																				
45																				
46																				
47																				
48																				
49																				
50																				
51																				
52																				
53																				
54																				
55																				
56																				
57																				
58																				
59																				
60																				
61																				
62																				
63																				
64																				
65																				
66																				
67																				
68																				

Congratulations! You have now finished the *First Aid for Reading* program.

What an excellent effort!

Vocabulary list

All of the following words are featured in *First Aid for Reading*. They include the sight words used in the book and the 400 words most commonly appearing in standard reading schemes. The total, over 2,500, covers all the most frequently used words in English.

a	are	battle	blender	breast	bustle	caution	choice	coins
about	arms	bay	blinds	breath	busy	cavern	choke	cold
above	around	be	blister	breathes	but	celebrated	choking	collapsed
accident(s)	artist	beach	bloat	breeding	butterfly	celery	chooks	collected
ached	artistic	beachfront	blocked	breeze	button	cellar	choose	collection
action(s)	as	bead	blonde	brew	buy	cellophane	chop	collects
actors	ascent	beak(s)	blood	brick(s)	buying	cemetery	chopped	colorful
adore	ask	bear	blouse	bride	buzz	centipedes	chords	coloring
adventure	asleep	beast	blow	bridge	buzzing	century	chose	comb
afraid	astronauts	beat	blown	brief	by	certain	chowder	come
after	at	because	blue	briefcase	cab	chain	Christmas	comic(s)
again	ate	bed	blunt	briefly	cabin	chair	chugging	committed
age	athlete	beef	blush	bright	cage	chalk(s)	chunk(s)	competition
aground	athletics	been	boarding	brilliant	cake(s)	chameleon	church	complain
ahead	attached	beer	boards	brim	call	champ(s)	churn	completed
air	attacked	bees	boast(s)	bring	calling	champion	cigarette(s)	cone
aircraft	attempt	before	boat	broke	came	championship	circle	confection
airless	attended	beginners	bodies	broken	camp	chance	city	continue
airport	attention	begs	bog	bronze	camping	change	clam	cook(s)
alarm	attic	behead	boil(s)	broom	can(s)	changed	clank	cooked
alien	August	belief	boiling	broth	can't	chap(s)	clash	cool
all	avoid	believe	bomb	brother	candle	chapel	claws	cop
along	away	bell(s)	bone	brought	canned	charm	clay	coral
alphabet	babies	bellowed	book	brown	cannonball	charmers	cleaning	cork
alter	baby	bench	boor	brush	cannot	chase	cliff	corner(s)
although	babysitting	bend	bored	brushes	cap	chased	climb	corny
always	back	bent	boss	brute	captain	chasing	climbing	cost
am	bacon	berry	botch	bubble	capture	chat	clinch	cot
amazing	bad	best	both	budge	captured	chatting	clippers	cotton
ambushed	badly	better	bottle	bug	carbon	cheap	cloak	couch
among	bag(s)	between	bottom	build	carcass	cheat	clock	cough
amount	bait	biff(s)	bough	buildings	cards	cheeky	clop	could
ample	bake	big	bought	bull	careful	cheeps	close(s)	count
amuse(s)	baker	bike(s)	boulder	bulldozer	carpet	cheese	cloth	counted
and	baking	bill	bounded	bullets	carrier	cheetah	clothed	counter
anger	bald	billion	bows	bullion	carries	chef	clothes	countries
angry	ball	billowed	box	bulls	carrion	chemicals	cloud(s)	country
animals	balloon(s)	bin	boxing	bun(s)	carrot(s)	chemist	cloudy	couple(s)
ankle	balls	binge	boy(s)	bunch	carry	chemistry	clown('s)	coupon
annoy	ban	bips	brain	bunk	cart	chess	clowned	courage
annoyed	band	bird(s)	branch	burger	carton	chest	club	court
another	bang	birthday	branches	burglars	carve	chew	clucking	cousin
ant(s)	banisters	biscuits	brand	burning	carving	chicken	clue	cover
any	bank	bit(s)	brash	burns	cash	chief	clutch	cow(s)
appeared	banned	bite	brat	burned	castle	children	clutches	crab
appearing	banquet	bitter	brave	burrows	cat	chill	coach	crack
applauded	bare	black	braver	burst	catch	chime	coast	cracked
apple	bark(s)	blackbirds	bravest	bursting	catches	chimney	coat	crackers
apply	barn	blackboard	brawling	bus	caterpillar	chimp(s)	cocker	cracking
applying	basketball	blacker	brawn	bush	cattle	chin	spaniel	cram
apricots	bat	blackest	bread	bushed	caught	chink	code	crane
April	batch	blamed	breakfast	bushes	cause	chips	coffee	crank
arch	bath	bleed	breaking	bust	caused	chocolate	coils	crash

crashed	day	downstairs	enclosure	feet	flow	furnace	grapes	have
crates	dead	doze	end(s)	fell	flowers	furniture	grass	hawk(s)
crawling	deadly	dozen	engine	felon(s)	flowery	furry	grate	hay
crayfish	deaf	dragon	enjoy	fence	fluffy	further	grated	he
crazy	decided	drain	enjoyed	feral	fluke(s)	fuse(s)	gravestone	healthy
cream	deck	drank	enormous	ferns	flute	future	gravy	heap
crease	deep	draw	enough	ferry	fly	gain	grazing	heard
creeps	deer	drawn	equal	fertilizer	flying	gamble	grease	hearing
crept	delay	dread	escaped	fetch	foam	gambler	great	heat
crew	delighted	dreadful	event	few	fog	game	greedy	heated
cricket	delightful	dream	every	fiction	foil	garage	green	heavy
cried	delivered	dreamed	everyone	fielded	fold	garden	greet	hedge
crime	den	drenches	everywhere	fields	footsteps	gardener	grief	hedgehog
croaking	dentures	dried	evidence	fig(s)	footy	gas	grieved	heel
crocodiles	department	drifted	exact	fill	for	gate	grinds	held
crooks	departs	drink(s)	excellent	filled	forecast	gave	grip	helicopter
crop(s)	descends	drips	exchange	fin	forest	geese	groaned	hello
cross	design	drive(s)	exciting	final	forged	general	groaning	help
crossroads	desk	driver	excuses	finch	forgot	generator	groom	helped
crow	destroy	driving	exhausted	find	fork	generous	ground(s)	hem
crowded	dew	drop	expect	fine	fort	genie	group	hen(s)
crown	dice	dropped	expensive	finger	fortress	genius	grouse	her
crowned	dictionary	drove	exploded	fir	fortune	gentle	grove	here
cruellest	did	drowned	explored	fire	fought	germs	growling	hid
cruise	different	drug	explosion	fired	found	get	grown	hidden
crumble	dig	drum	extremely	first	fountain	ghost(s)	grows	high(s)
crumbs	digger	drummers	eye(s)	fish	four	giant	grumpy	hill(s)
crush	digging	drunk	eyedropper	fisherman	fourteenth	gigantic	guard(s)	him
crushes	dill	dry	fable	fishing	fourth	giraffe	guess	himself
crust(s)	dine	drying	fabulous	fist	fox	girls	guest(s)	hinge
crutches	ding	duck	face	fit	foxes	give	guilty	hippo
cry	dining	duff	factory	five	fraction	glad	guinea pig	hired
crystal	dinner	dug	fad	fix	fractured	glide	guitar	his
crystal ball	dirt	dump	fade	fixture	frail	gloated	gum	hiss
cub	disappointing	dunce	fail	fizz	frame	glove(s)	gun	hit
cube(s)	disco	dunes	failed	flag	frank	glow	gunfire	hive
cuff(s)	discover	dungeon	faint	flair	free	glue	gunners	hoard(s)
cuffed	dish	dunny	fair	flames	freight	glutton	guy	hobby
cunning	disk	dust	fairer	flan	frequent	gnashes	had	hoes
cup	dislodged	dusty	fairest	flare(s)	fresh	gnat(s)	hair	hoist
curious	display	eagle(s)	fairly	flared	friction	gnaw(s)	hairless	hold
curls	distance	earl	fairy	flat	fridge	gnawed	hairy	holiday(s)
curly	disturb	earlier	falcons	flaws	fried	gnome	hall	hollow
cut	ditch	earth	fall(s)	flesh	friend	go	Halloween	home
cute	dive	earwigs	fallen	flew	frightful	goat(s)	ham	homework
cuter	diving	easier	family	flickered	frog(s)	gob	hammer(s)	honest
cutest	do	eat	famous	flies	from	gobbled	hand	honey
cyclones	dobbers	eaten	fan	flight	front	goes	handle	honeymoon
dad	does	eating	fangs	fling	frost	going	handlebars	hood
daily	dog(s)	echoed	far	flipped	froth	go-karts	hang	hook
dairy	doll(s)	edge(s)	fare	flippers	frowned	gold	happened	hooters
dam	dollars	eggs	farm	float	fruit juice	golden	hard	hop
damage	dolly	eight	farmer(s)	floated	frustrated	golf	hare(s)	hope
damp	dome	eighteen	fast	floating	fudge	gong	harm	hopping
dance	don't	eighteenth	faster	flood(s)	full	good	has	horn(s)
dangerous	done	eighty	fastest	flooded	fumes	got	hat	horse(s)
dare	donkey(s)	electric	fat	floor	fun	gown	hatch	hose
dared	door	elephant(s)	father	floorboards	funeral	grab	hatchlings	hospital
dark	dork	embers	fears	flop	funny	graceful	haul	hostess
darn	doubles	emergency	feature	floppy	fur	grade	hauled	hot
daughter	dove	empty	fed	flour	furious	grain	hauling	hour(s)
dawn	down	emus	fee	flourish	furls	grand	haunted	house

households	joint	laugh	loose	men	mute	offering	paw	plover
how	jokes	laughed	loot	mend	mutt	office	pawns	plucking
howls	joy	laughing	lose	mention	mutton	officer(s)	pay	plum
huddle	jug(s)	launch	loser	mess	my	oil	paying	plunged
huge	juicer	launched	lost	met	myself	oinks	pea	plush
hundred	juke	launder	lot(s)	mice	mystery	ointment	peach	poach
hung	jukebox	laundry	lotion	middle	myth(s)	old	peaches	poacher
hungry	July	law	loud	might	nag	on	pearl(s)	pocket
hunters	jump	lawn	loudly	milk	nail(s)	once	peas	pod(s)
hunting	jumper	lazy	lounge	mill	nap	one	peg(s)	point
hurled	June	lead	lout	million	nappy	only	pelican	pointed
hurry	junk	leak(s)	love	mind	narrow	open	pen(s)	poise
hurt	just	leaking	lover	mine	national	or	pencils	poison
hut(s)	kangaroos	lean	loyal	mini	native	orange(s)	pension	poisonous
hutch	keep	learn	lucky	mint	natural	ordered	people	poke(s)
I	kept	least	luminous	miss	naught	orphan	pepper	poked
I've	kettle	leather	lunch	missing	naughty	orphaned	perilous	police
ice	keys	leave(s)	lunged	mist	nearby	other	permission	polish
ice-cream	kick	leaving	machine	mite	neat	our(s)	pest	polite
icy	kid	lecture	mad	mix	necessary	ourselves	pet(s)	pond
idiot	kill	lectured	madder	mixture	neck	out	phantom	pongs
if	killed	ledge	made	moan	need(s)	outside	pheasant	pool
ignored	kind	left	magazine	moat	neigh	over	phone	pop
important	kindergarten	leg(s)	maggots	moist	neighed	overcast	photo	poppies
impressed	king	lemon(s)	magic	Monday	nervous	overflowed	photograph	popular
imprisonment	kiosk	less	mail	money	nest	overhaul	photography	porch
improve	kiss	let(s)	mailed	monkey(s)	nested	owl(s)	piano	pork
improvement	kissed	letter(s)	main	monstrous	nesting	own	pick	porous
in	kitchen	lice	make	month(s)	net	owned	picking	port
indicated	kite	lid	maker	monthly	netball	oysters	picnic	position
infection(s)	kitten(s)	lied	making	moon	nettles	pace	picture(s)	possums
injection	kiwi	life	mall	mops	never	packets	pie	post
ink	knack	lift	malt	morning	new	paddle	pig(s)	posture
innings	knapsack	lifting	mammals	moss	news	paddled	piggy	pot(s)
insects	knee	light	man	most	next	paddock	pigsty	pouch
inside	knife	lightning	mane	moth	nib	page	pile	pour
install	knight	like(s)	mansion	mother	nice	paid	pill(s)	pouring
instead	knit(s)	limb	many	motorbike	nicest	pail	pin(s)	pout
instructions	knock	lime	map	mould	night	pain	pinch	powder
interesting	knocked	limit	marathon	mouldier	nine	paint	pink	practice
interrupted	knots	limp	marble	mouldy	ninth	painted	pipe	pram
into	know	line(s)	march	mountain(s)	nips	painting	pith	prance
invention	koala(s)	lions	marched	mourned	no	pair(s)	pizza(s)	prank
invited	lace	lip(s)	mare	mouse	nocturnal	pamphlets	place	praying
iron(s)	laced	liquid	market	move(s)	noise	pan(s)	placed	prefer
is	ladder	listen	marks	movie	noodles	panther	plain	present(s)
it(s)	lady	lit	married	mow	nose	pantry	plan	prettier
itching	laid	little	marshmallows	much	not	pants	plane	pretty
itchy	lair(s)	live	marvellous	mud	notes	parachute	plank(s)	prevent
jack	lake	liver	mass	muddle	notions	parks	plant(s)	prey
jacket	lamb	lizard	mat	muddy	nourish	parsnip	planting	price
jaguar	lamp	load	match	muffins	now	parts	plastic	prickled
jam	landslide	loam	matching	mug(s)	number	party	plate(s)	prickly
jaws	lap	lock(s)	mate	mule(s)	nut(s)	pass	platform	pride
jealous	large	locked	mattress	mum	o'clock	past	platter	priest
jeans	lark(s)	log(s)	may	mumbled	oar(s)	pasture(s)	platypus	prince
jelly	lash	lollies	me	munching	obedient	pat	play(s)	princess
jet	lass	lolly	meat	murder	obey	patch	playful	print
jewels	last	London	meet	murderer	of	patching	playground	prize
job	latch	long	meeting	mushrooms	off	path	playing	problems
joey	late	longer	melon(s)	music	offered	paunch	please	prod
join	later	look(s)	melted	must		pause	plenty	produces

project	rap	rob	scraps	shorts	sliced	sorry	stalked	stronger
property	rapture	robber(s)	scratch	shot	slide(s)	sought	stalking	struck
protect	rare	robbery	screamed	should	sliders	sound	stalks	stuck
prove(s)	rash	robin	sculpture	shoulder	sliding	sounded	stall	studio
provided	rat	rod	scurries	shoulders	slim	sour	stallion	stuffy
prowled	rate	rode	scurry	shouting	slime	south	stamp(s)	stumbled
prune	rather	roll(s)	sea	shove	slip	soy	stance	stunt
pruned	raw	roller	seals	shoved	slipped	spacecraft	stand	such
pub	rays	ropes	seam	shovelled	slippers	spaceship	stare	sucked
pudding	reach	rose(s)	season	show	slippery	spanners	start(s)	sued
puddle(s)	read	rotten	seasoning	showers	slipping	spared	startled	sugar
puff(s)	real	rough	seats	shrieked	slop	spark	station	suit
puffed	reason	round	second	shrubs	slope	sparkling	statues	sum(s)
puke	recipe	route	secret	shut	sloppy	sparrow(s)	stay	summer(s)
pull(s)	recover	row	see(s)	shuttle	slot	special	stayed	sun('s)
pulled	recovered	royal	seedlings	shy	slow	speed	steak	Sunday
pullover	recruit	rub	seeks	sick	slowed	spent	steam	sunny
pump	red	rubbed	seem	sicker	slum	spew	steamed	sunscreen
pumpkin	reduction	rubber	seen	sideboard	slush	spice	steel	super
punch	reef	rubbish	selection	sides	small	spider(s)	steep	supermarket(s)
puncture	reeks	rude	sell(s)	sighs	smaller	spies	stench	supper
punished	refreshing	rudest	sent	sight	smallest	spilt	stepladder	supplies
pup(s)	refuse(s)	rug	sentenced	sign	smart	spin	stew	supply
puppies	refused	rule	sequins	sill	smarty	spitting	stewed	sure
puppy	relay	rum	serious	silly	smash	splash	stick(s)	surface
purple	released	run(s)	sermon	silver	smell	splashing	stickers	surgery
pushed	relief	rung	service	silverfish	smelly	spoil	sticky	swallow
put	relieved	runners	set	since	smile	spoiled	stile	swallowed
putt	reliever	rush	seven	sing	smoking	spoke(s)	still	swans
putted	rely	rust	several	sink	smother	spoken	sting	swap
quack	remove	rusty	sew	sip	smoulder	sponge	stinging	swapped
quacking	repair(s)	safety	shakes	siren	snack	spool	stitch	swearing
queen	repairing	sage	shall	sister(s)	snail(s)	spoor	stocking	sweat
queer	replaced	said	shallow	sit	snake(s)	sports	stockman	sweater
quick	replied	sail	shape	sitting	snap	spot	stoked	sweep
quilt	reply	sailed	shared	six	snare(s)	spotted	stole	sweet(s)
quins	reports	sailing	shares	sixteen	snatch	spout	stolen	swept
quit(s)	required	sale	shark	sixty	snatched	spouting	stomp	swim
quite	rescued	salt	sharp	skates	sneaks	sprained	stomped	swimming
quiz	rest	salty	sharpen	skeletons	sniffle	spray	stone	swing(s)
rabbit	retriever	salute	she	sketch	snorkel	spraying	stood	swinging
rabbits	returned	same	shed	skewer	snout(s)	spread	stool	swish
race(s)	ribbon	sand	sheep	skidded	snow	spring	stooped	switch
raced	rice	sandwiches	sheet(s)	skies	snowballs	sprouts	stop	swooped
racing	rich	sat	shelf	skin	snowman	spy	stopped	swooping
rack	rickety	sauce	shells	skipper	snowy	squash	store	tag
radiant	rid	saucepans	shelter	skipping	snuggle	squeaked	stories	tail
radio	ride(s)	saw	shelve	skippy	so	squeaking	stout	take
radium	rider	say	shielded	sky	soak	squeaks	stove	taken
rafter(s)	riding	scale(s)	shift	slack	soaked	squeeze	stow	talk
rag	rifle	scamp	shine	slain	soap	squirted	strain	tall
rage	right	scared	shining	slant	socks	squirts	strange	taller
raided	rind	scarf	ship(s)	slap	soft	stables	stranger	tame
railway	ring	scary	shipwrecks	slash	soil	stack	stray	tan
rain	rinse	scenery	shirt(s)	slate	soiled	stadium	stream	tap
raised	rip(s)	scent	shook	slaughter	some	stage	streets	tape
rake	ripe	school	shooters	slay	something	stain	stretch	tart
ram(s)	river	science	shop(s)	sleep	sometimes	stainless	strewn	tasted
ran	riverbank	scissors	shoplift	sleet	son(s)	stair	string	tastes
ranch	road	scope	shopping	sleigh	song(s)	staircase	stripped	taught
rang	roars	scotch	short	slept	soon	stake	stroking	taunted
ranger	roast	scouts	shortly	slice(s)	sore(s)	stale	strong	tea

teacher	thirteen	tip	trailer	turnstile	vet	we	will	wrapping
teaching	thirty	tired	train	twelve	victims	wealthy	wilt	wreath
team	this	to	training	twenty	video(s)	wear	wilting	wreck
teapot	thistles	toads	tram	twice	village	weather	win	wrecked
tears	thorns	toadstools	tramp	twine	villagers	wedding	wince	wren
tease	those	toast	trap(s)	two	visitors	weighed	window	wrench
teaspoon	thought	toaster	trapped	umpire	volleyball	weight	wine	wrenched
teenagers	thoughtful	today	trash	unable	vultures	weird	winning	wrestle
teeth	thousand(s)	toddlers	trawler	unattended	waddle	well	winter	wretch
television	thrash	toes	tray	uncle	waddled	went	wish	wriggle
tell	threading	together	treading	under	wage	were	wishing	wrinkled
tellers	threats	told	tree	understood	wags	wet	witch	wrist
temperature	three	toll	trenches	underwater	wait	whack(s)	with	write
ten	threw	tomato	trestle	unfair	waiter	whacking	without	written
tennis	thrice	tomb	trice	unfairly	waiting	whale(s)	wizard	wrong
tension	thrill	tone	tried	unglued	walk	what	wolf	wrote
tent	throb	tonight	trifle	unlucky	walked	wheat	woman	yacht
terrified	throne	tonnes	trim	unwise	wall(s)	wheel(s)	women	yards
terrify	through	too	trip	up	wallabies	wheelchairs	won	yawn(s)
texture	throughout	tool	troop	upon	wallet	when	won't	yeast
than	throw	tooth	trophies	urgency	wand	where	wonder	yell
thank	throwing	top	trophy	urgent	wander	which	wonderful	yellow
that	thrush	toss	trouble	us	wandering	whiff	wooden	yelp
the	thud	toucans	troupe	use(s)	want(s)	while	wool	yes
theft	thug	touch	trousers	used	wardrobe	whimper(s)	woollen	yesterday
their	thumbs	tough	trout	useful	warm	whip	words	yet
them	thump	tourist(s)	trove	useless	was	whippet	work(s)	yeti
then	thunder	tournament	truck	usually	wash	whiskers	workers	yields
there	thunderstorms	tow	true	ute	washing	whisking	worms	you
these	ticket(s)	towel(s)	trunk	valley	wasps	whisper	worst	young
they	ticking	town	trust	value	wasted	whistles	worth	your
thick	tie	toy(s)	try	van	watch	white(s)	would	yourself
thief	tiffs	trace	tub	vandals	watched	whiz	wouldn't	youth(s)
thieves	tiger	traced	tube(s)	velvet	water	who('s)	wound	youthful
thin	tighten	track	tuck	venomous	watermelon	why	wounded	yummy
things	till(s)	tracked	tumbled	venue	wattle	wicked	wounding	zebra
think	timber	traction	tune(s)	very	wax	wig	wrap	zip
third	time(s)	traffic	tunnel	vest	way(s)	wild	wrapped	zoo
thirsty	tin	trail	turkey					

Certificate of Completion

Congratulations

_____

on successfully completing the
First Aid for Reading program.

Well done!

Signed (tutor): _____

Date: _____